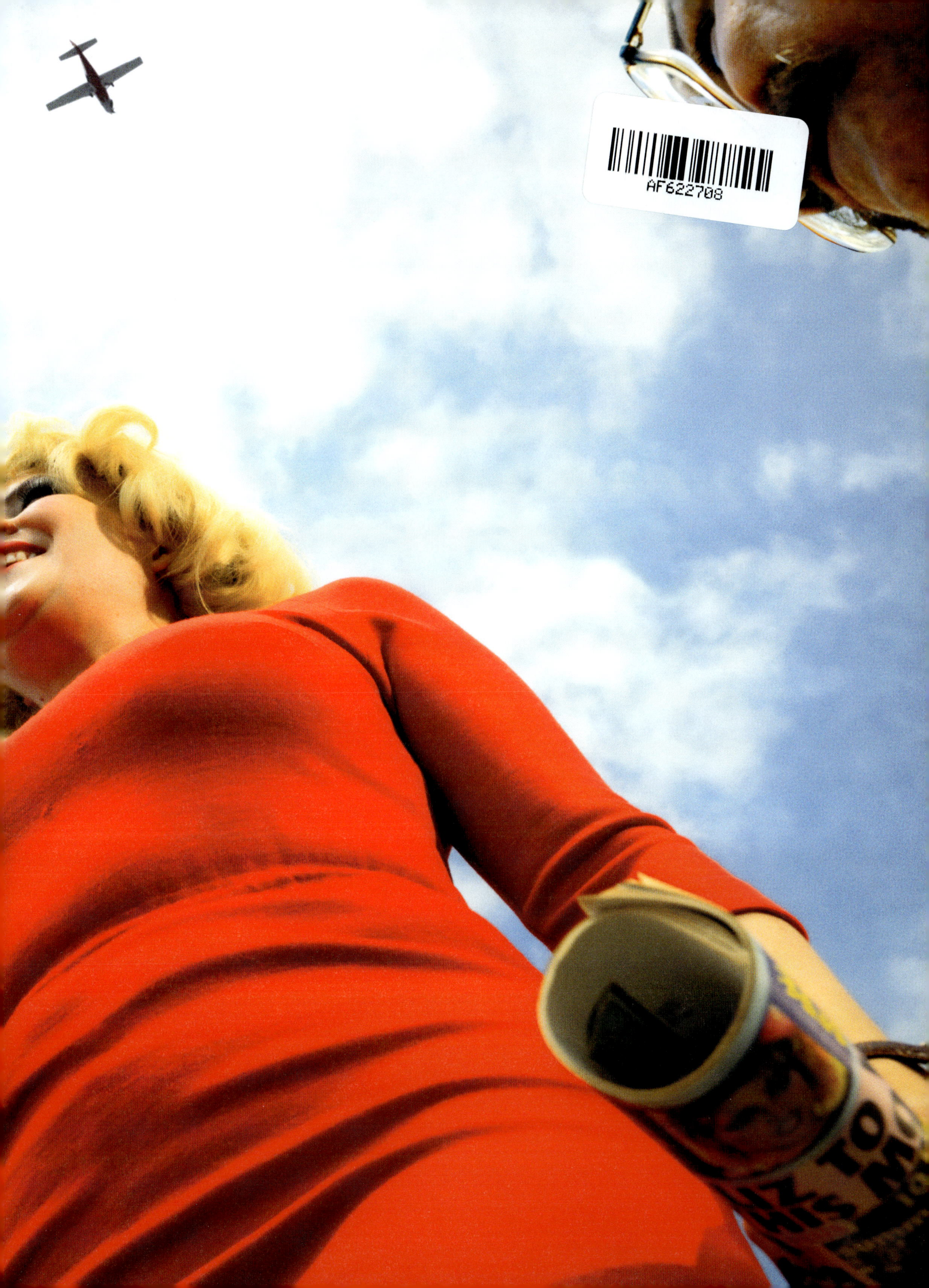

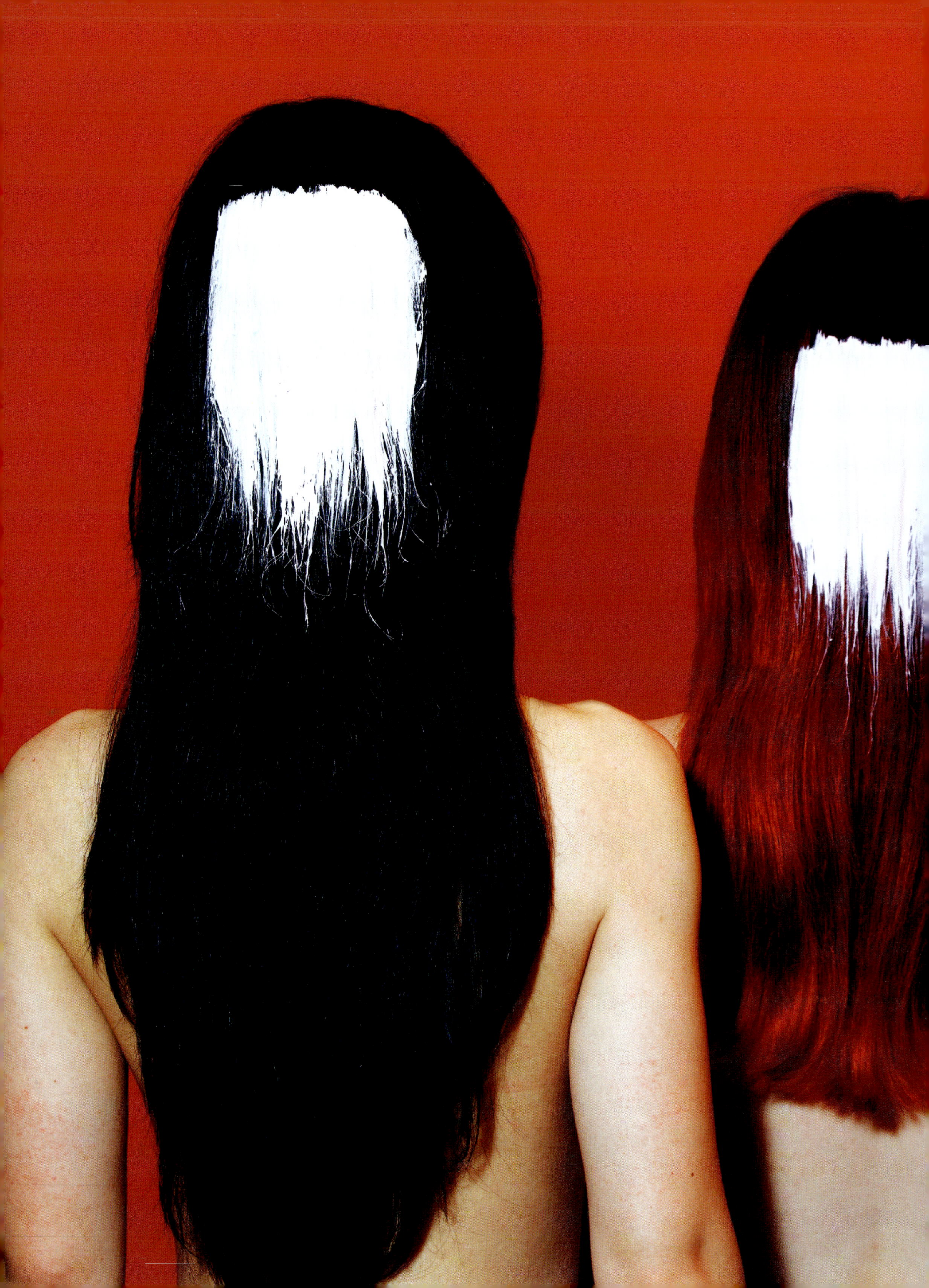

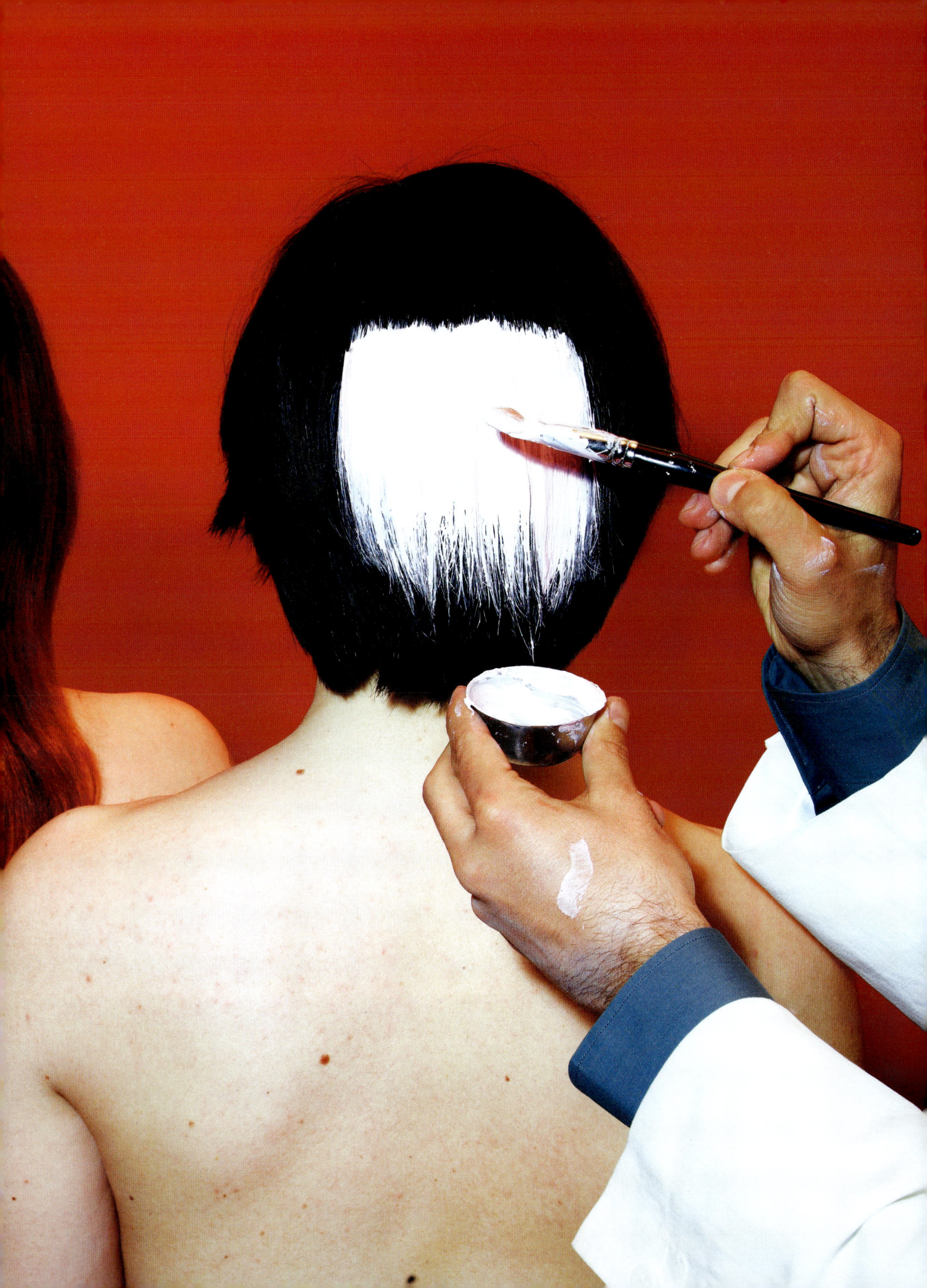

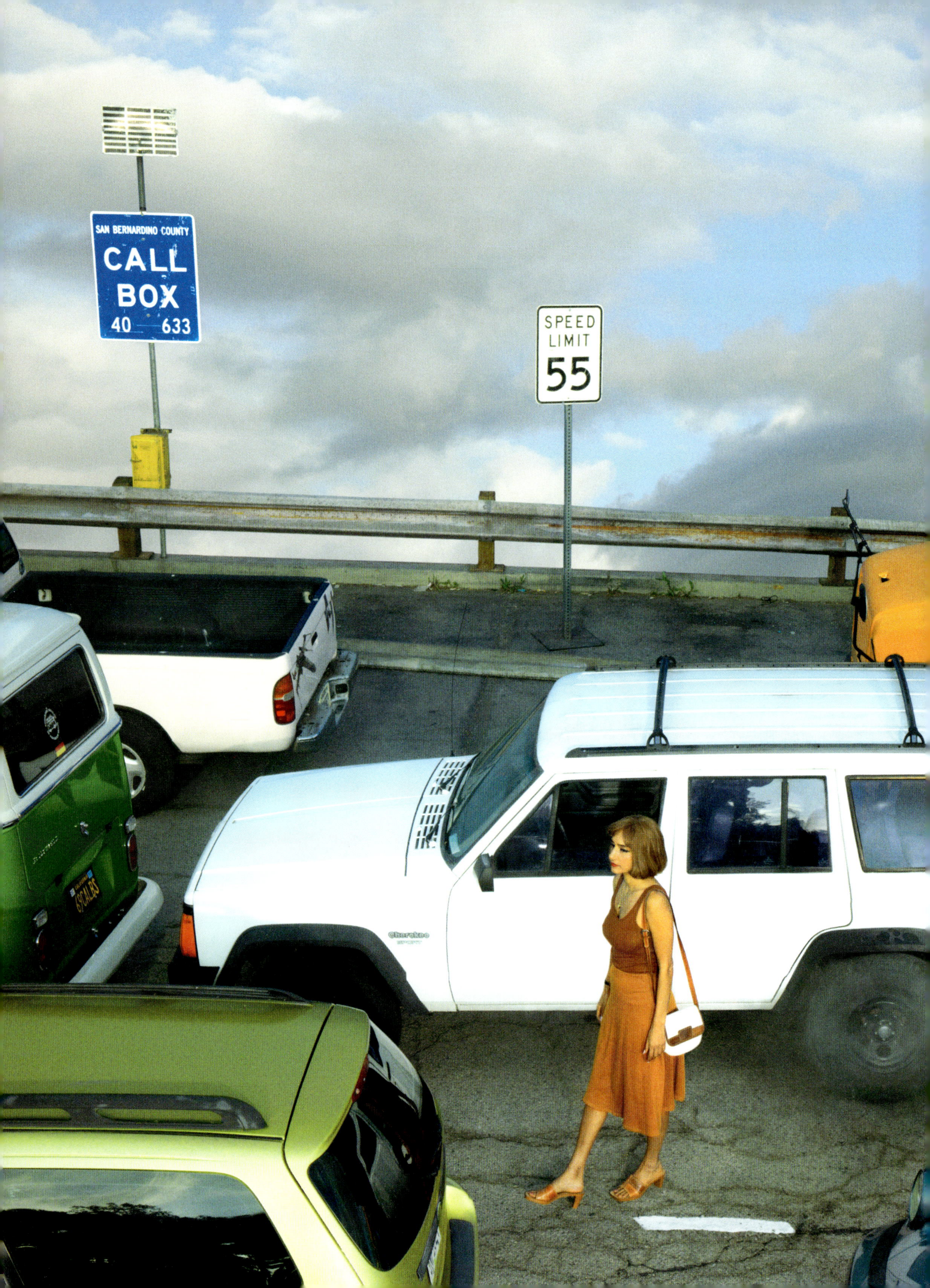
SAN BERNARDINO COUNTY
CALL
BOX
40 633
SPEED
LIMIT
55

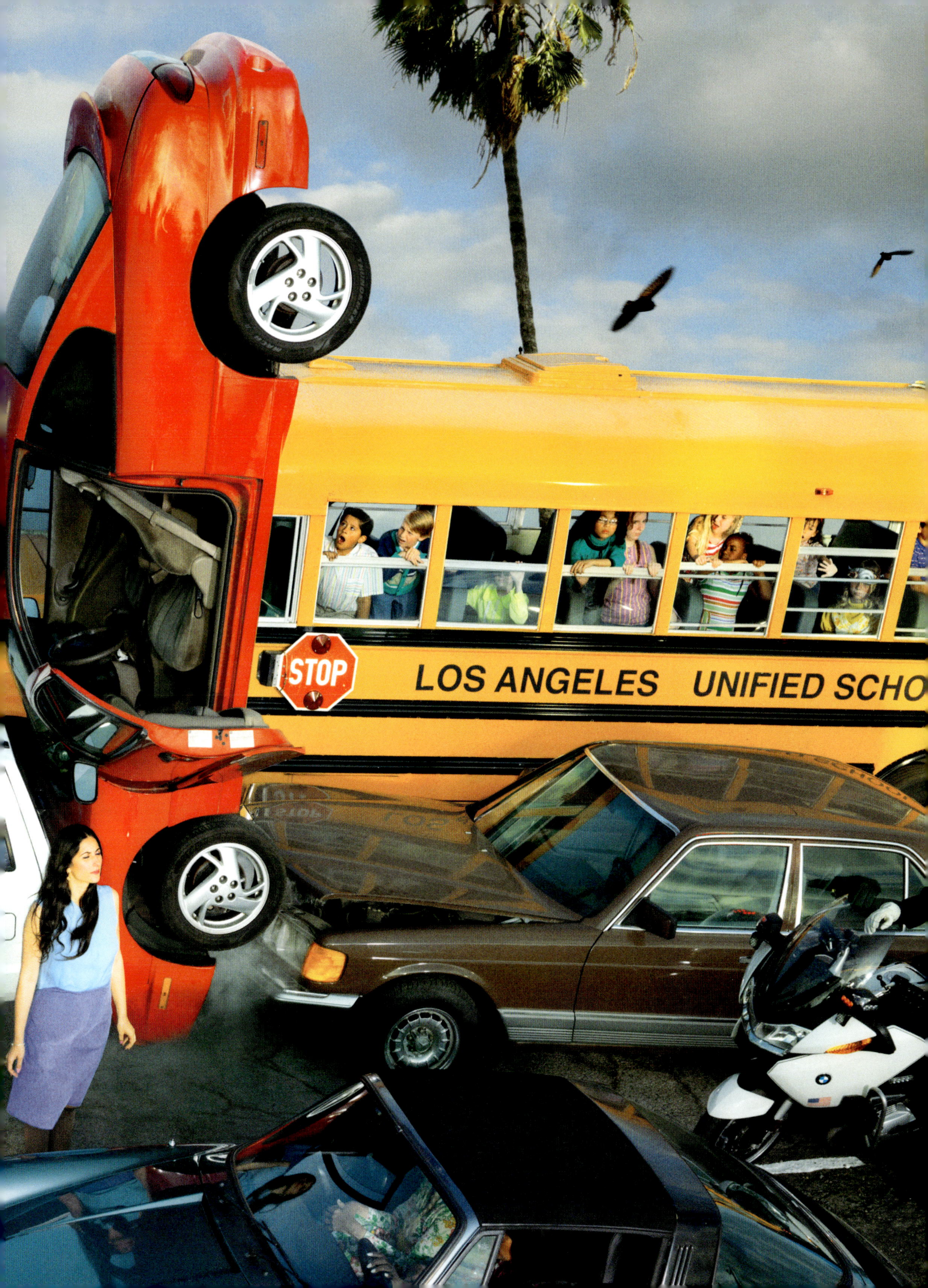
STOP
LOS ANGELES UNIFIED SCHO

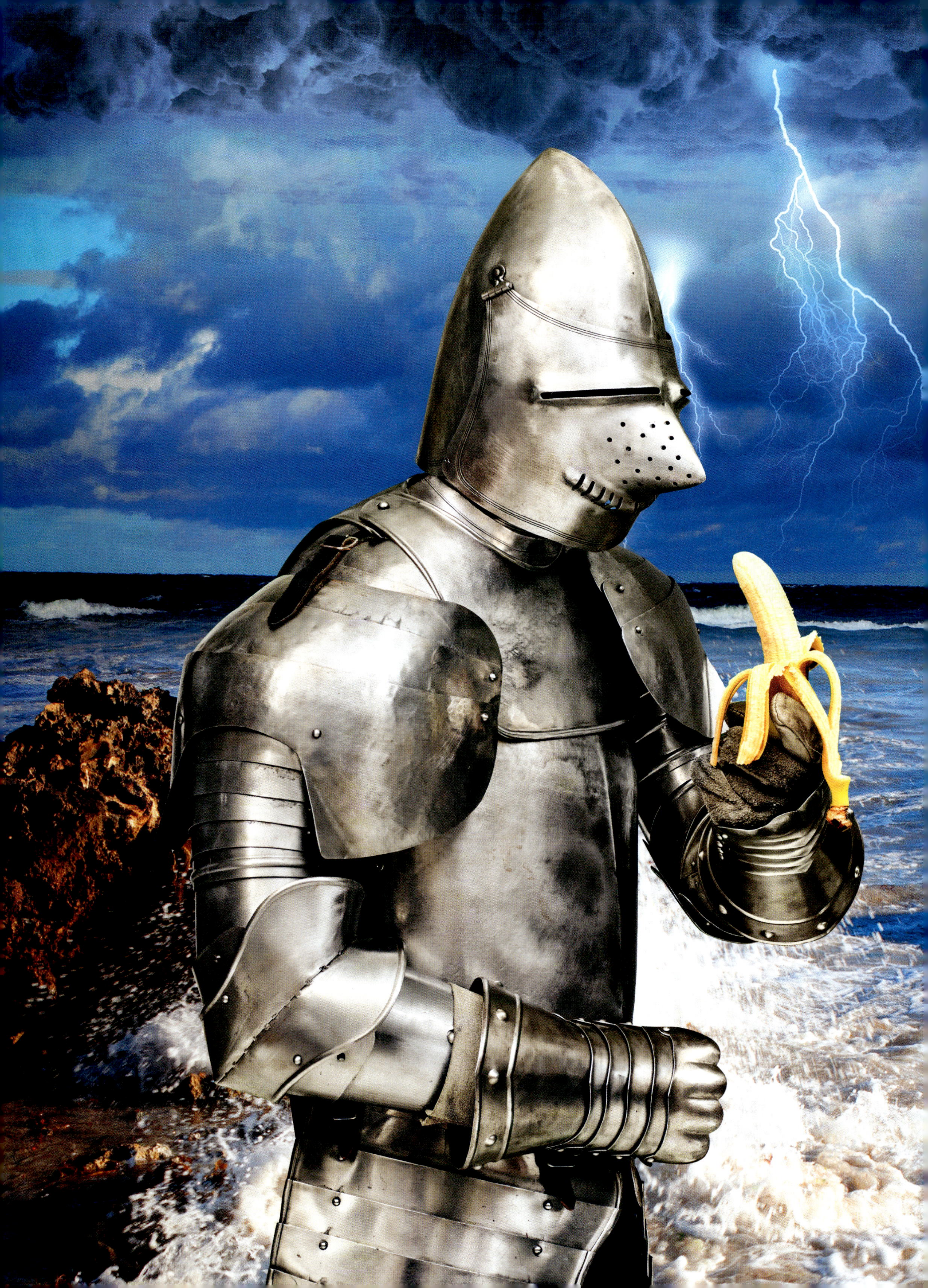

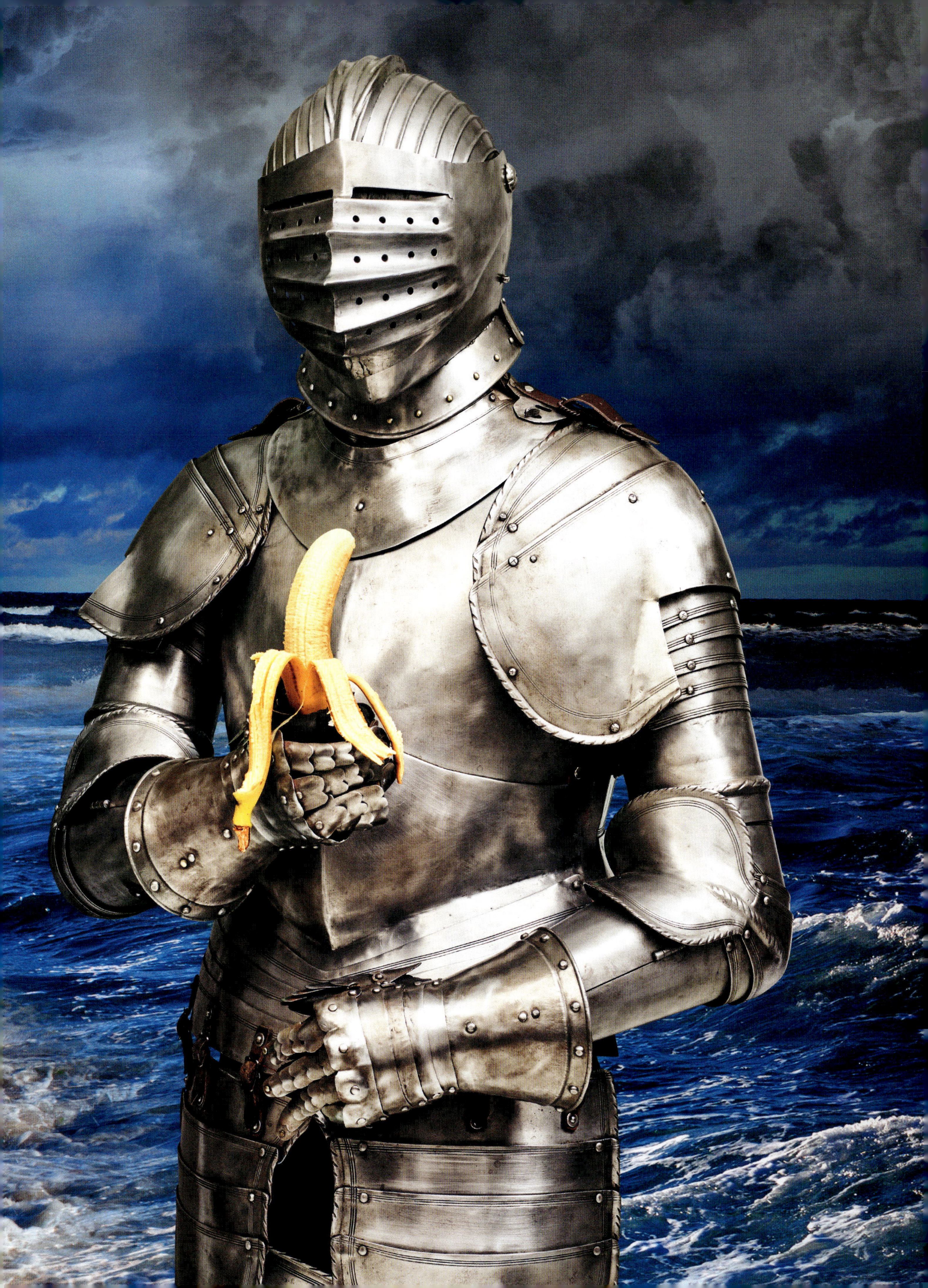

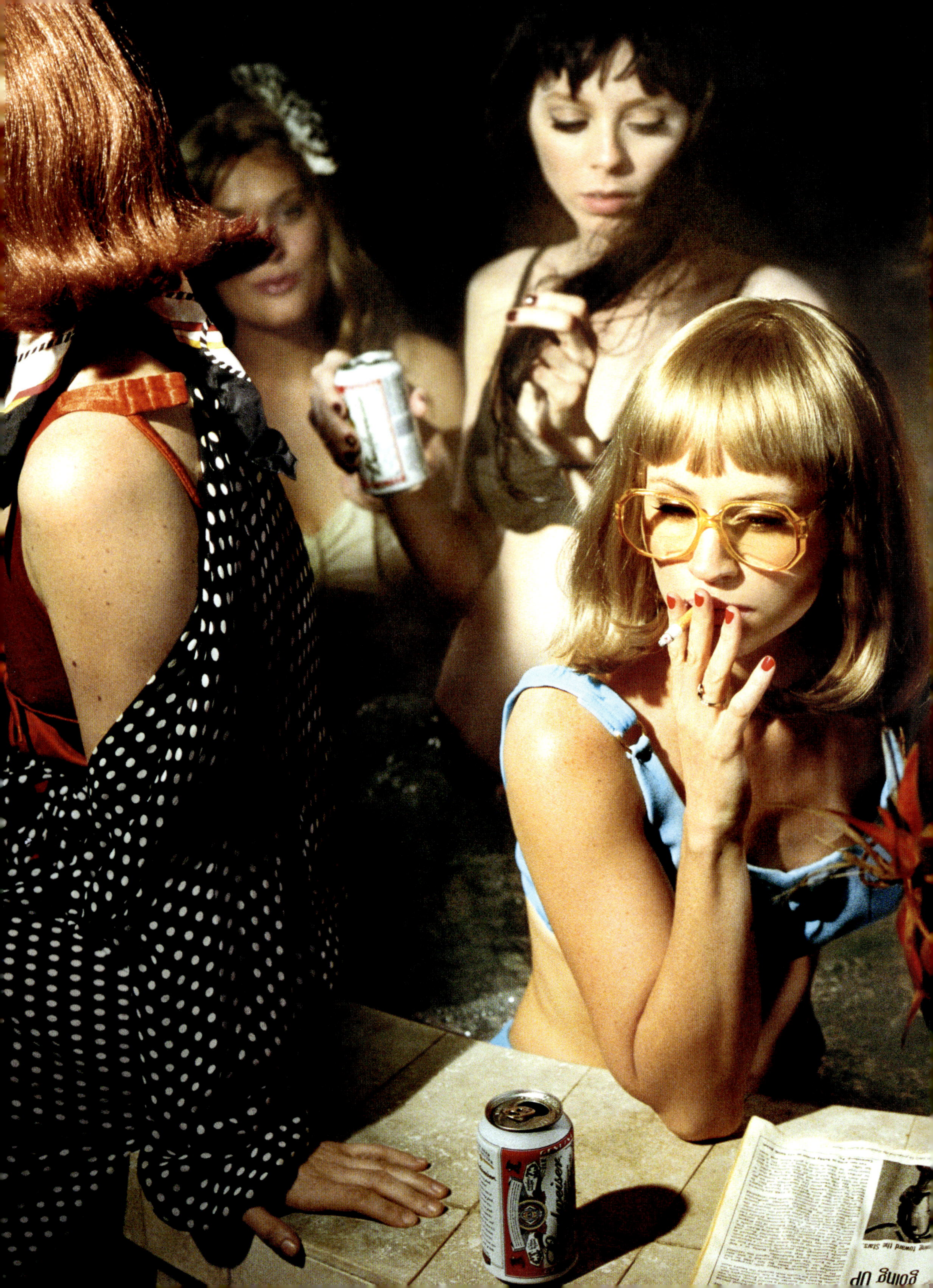

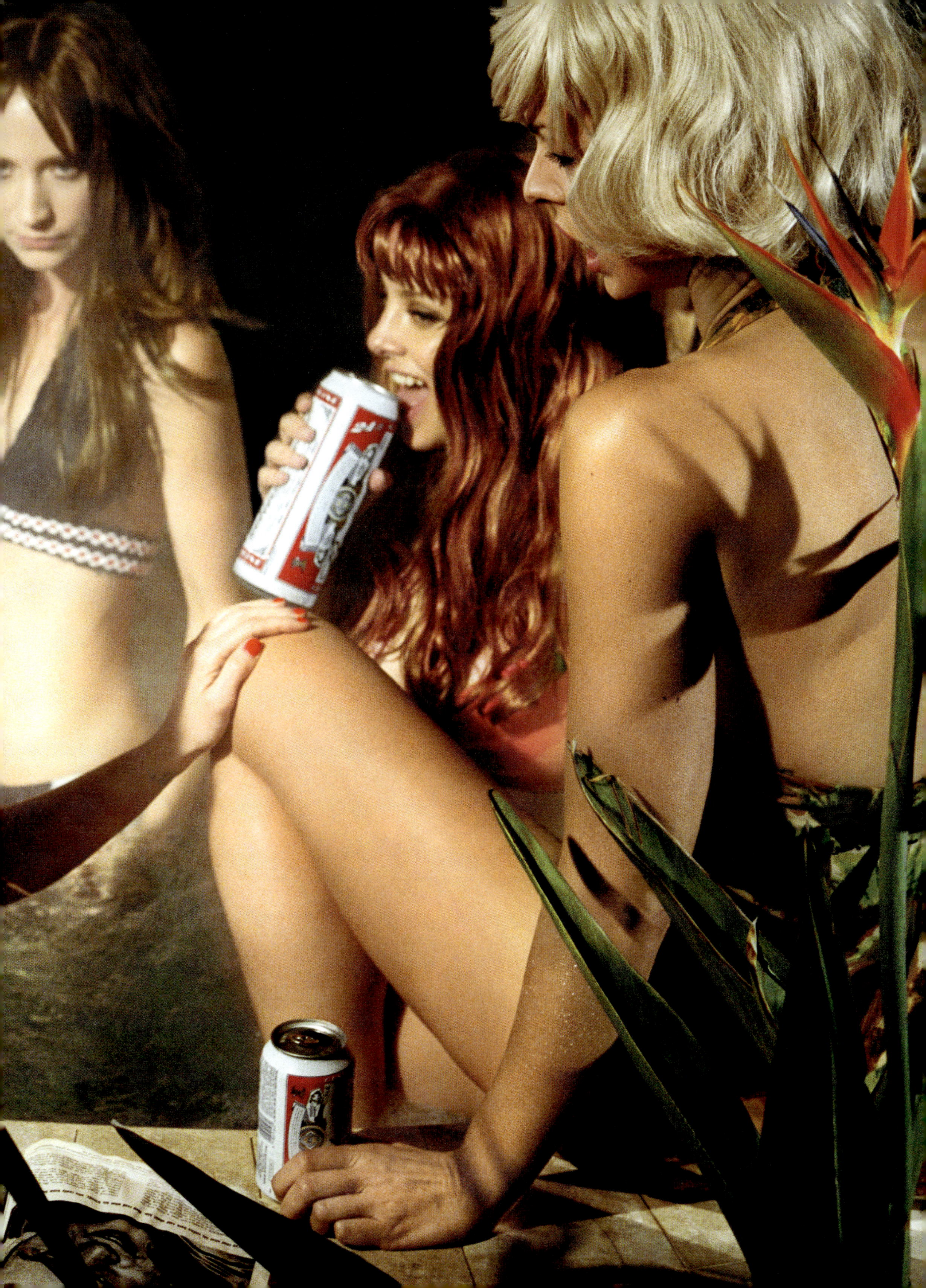

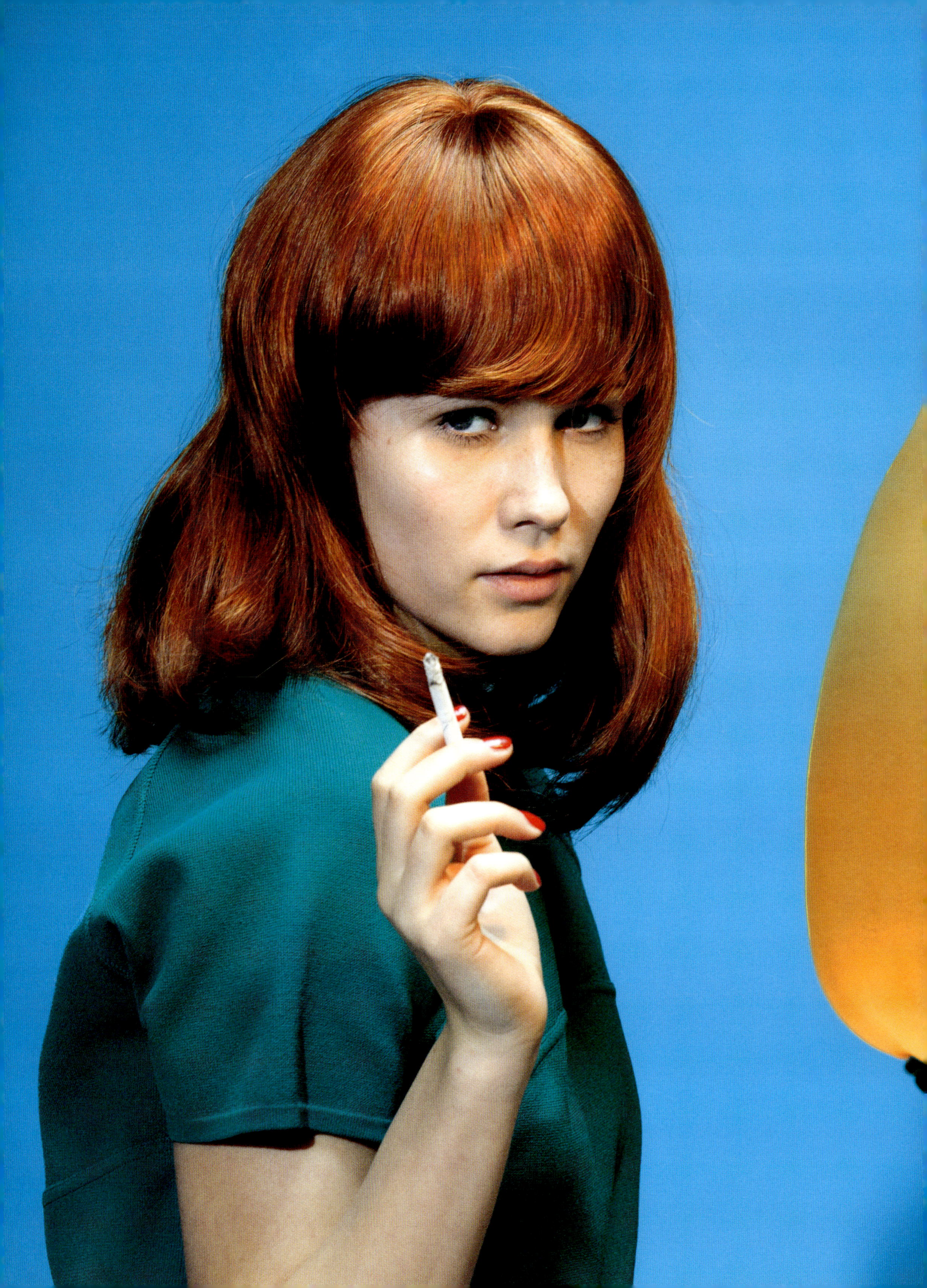

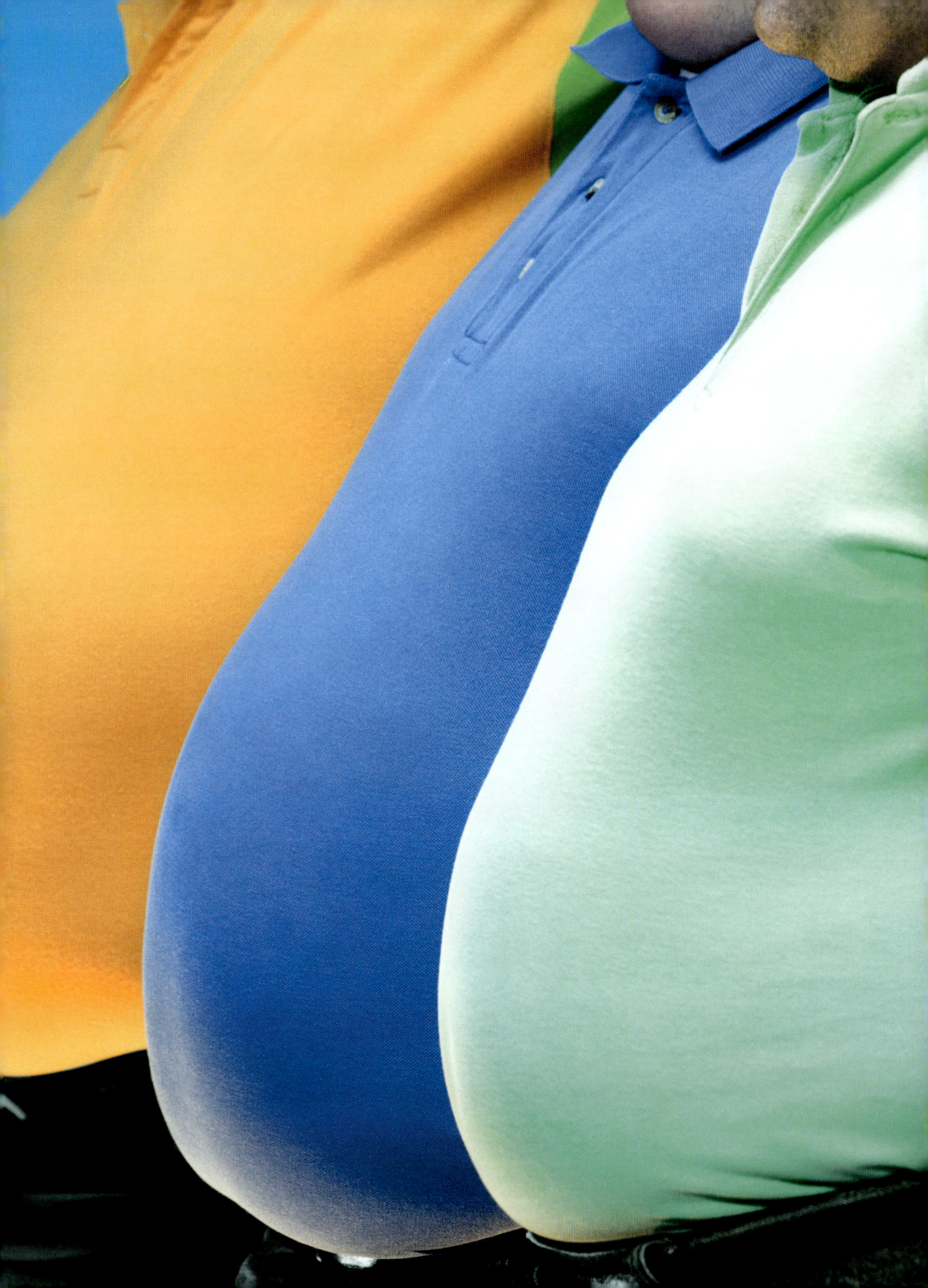

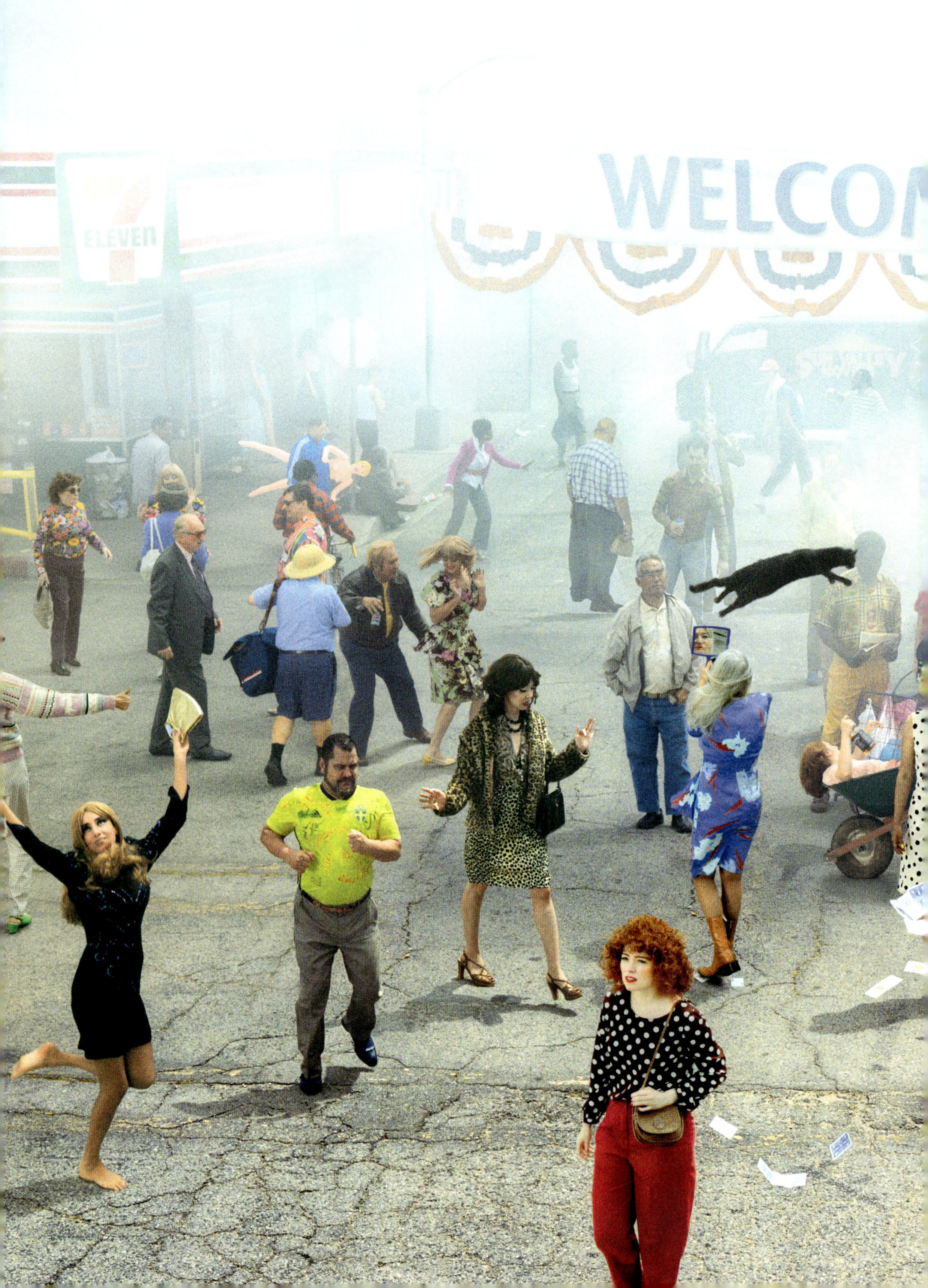
ELEVEN
WELCOM

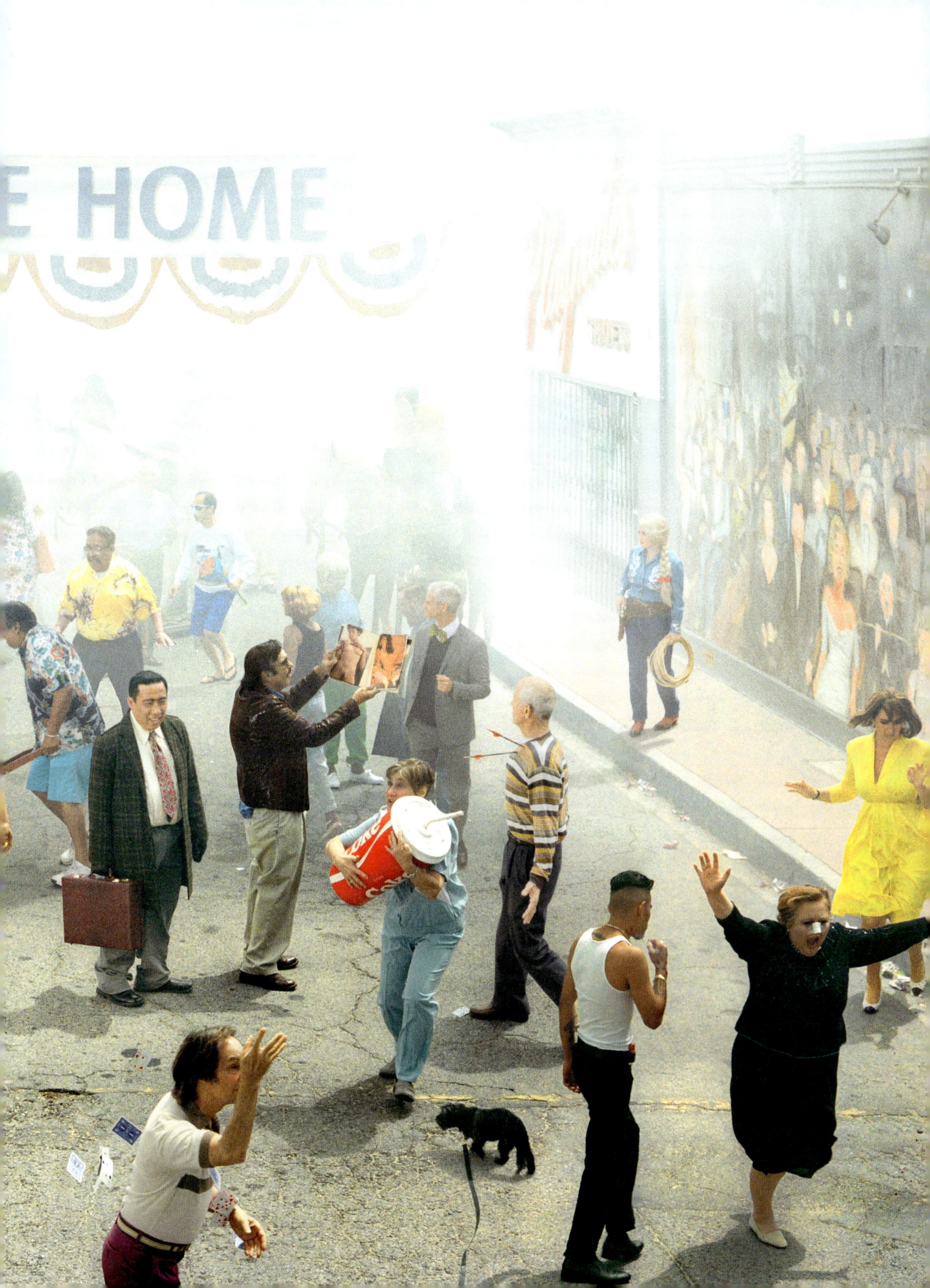
E HOME

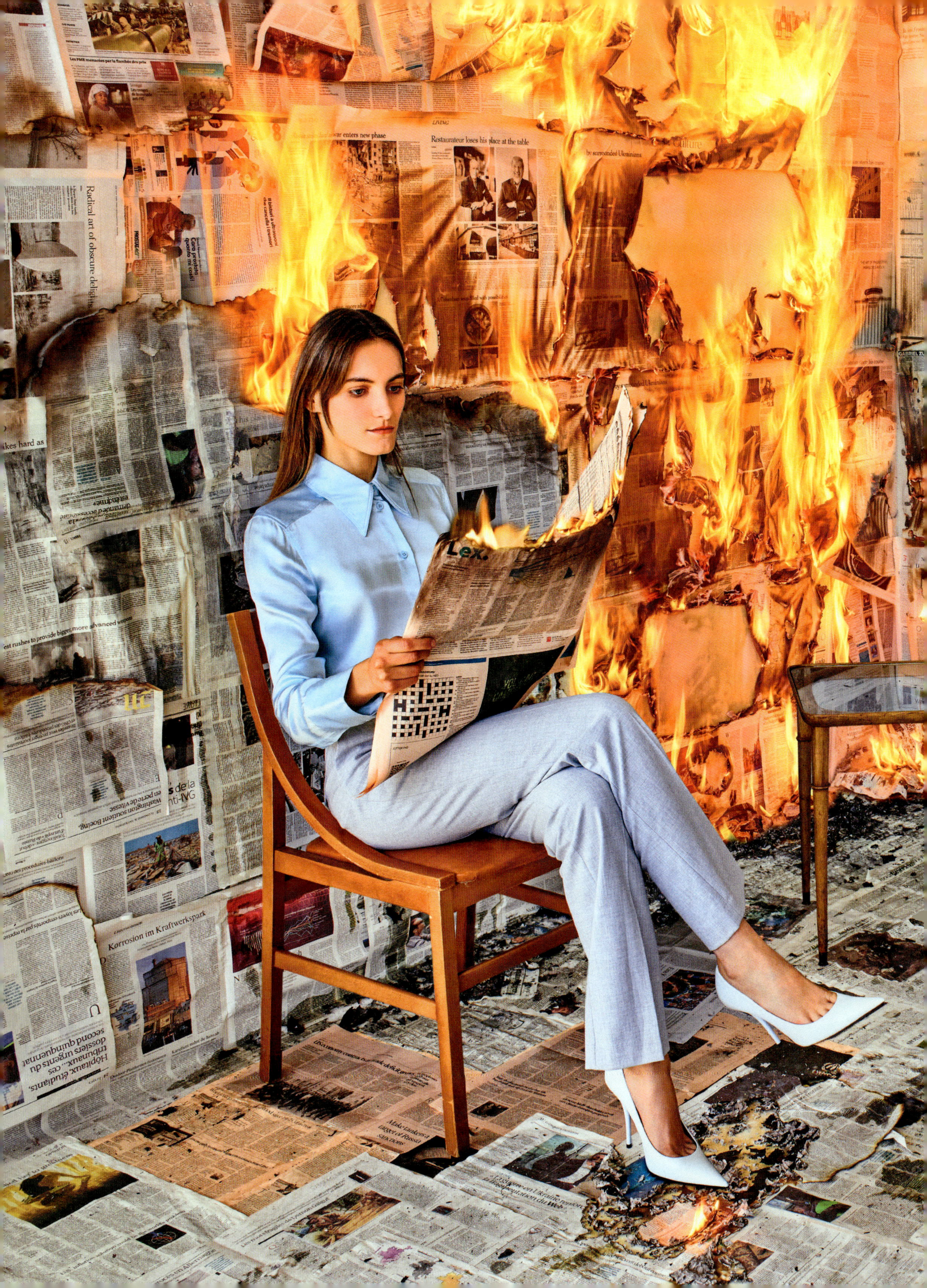
Restaurateur loses his place at the table
Radical art of obscure delight
Korrosion im Kraftwerkspark
Lex.

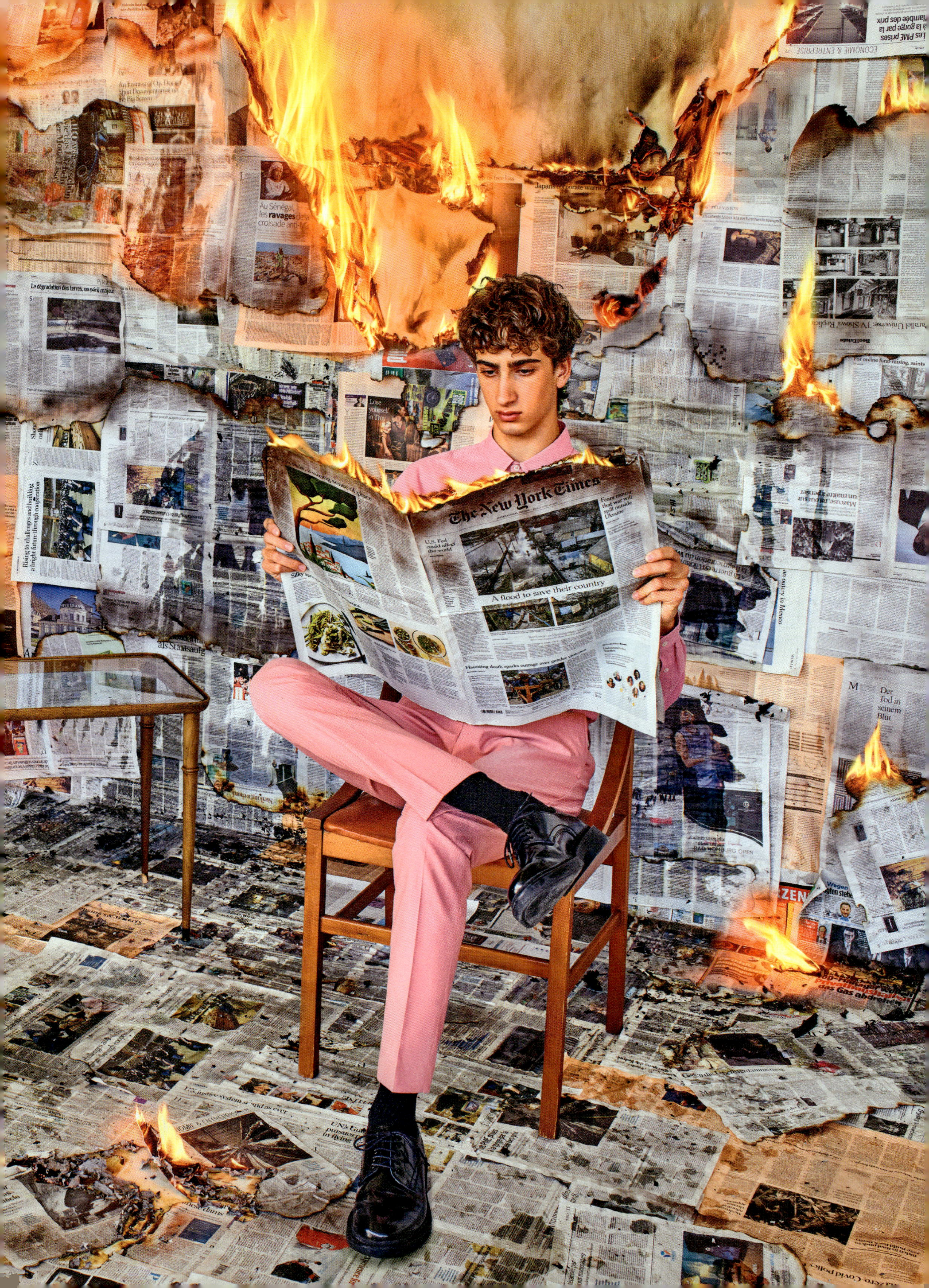

The New York Times
A flood to save their country
Rising to challenges and building a bright future through cooperation
Der Tod in seinem Blut

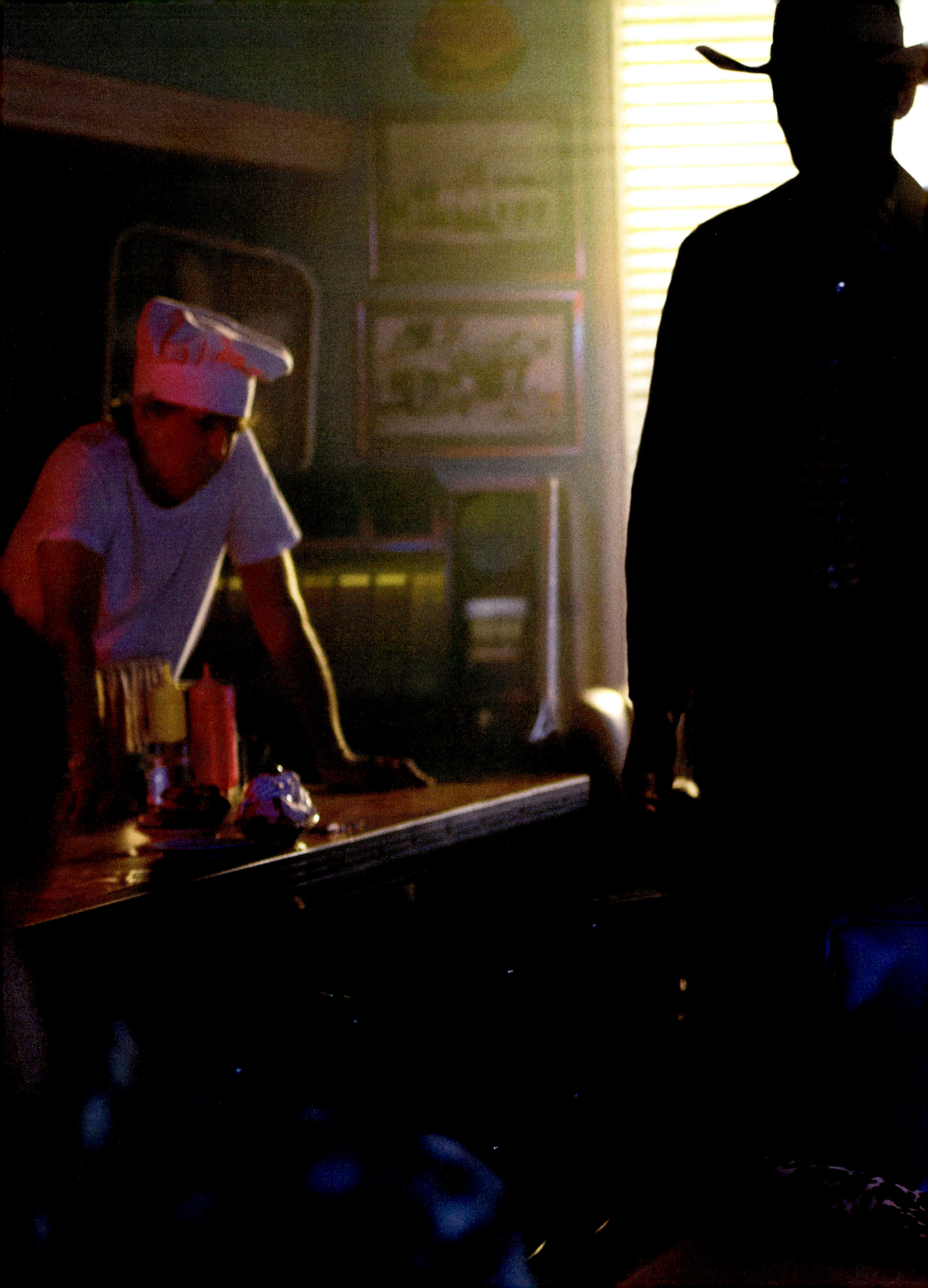

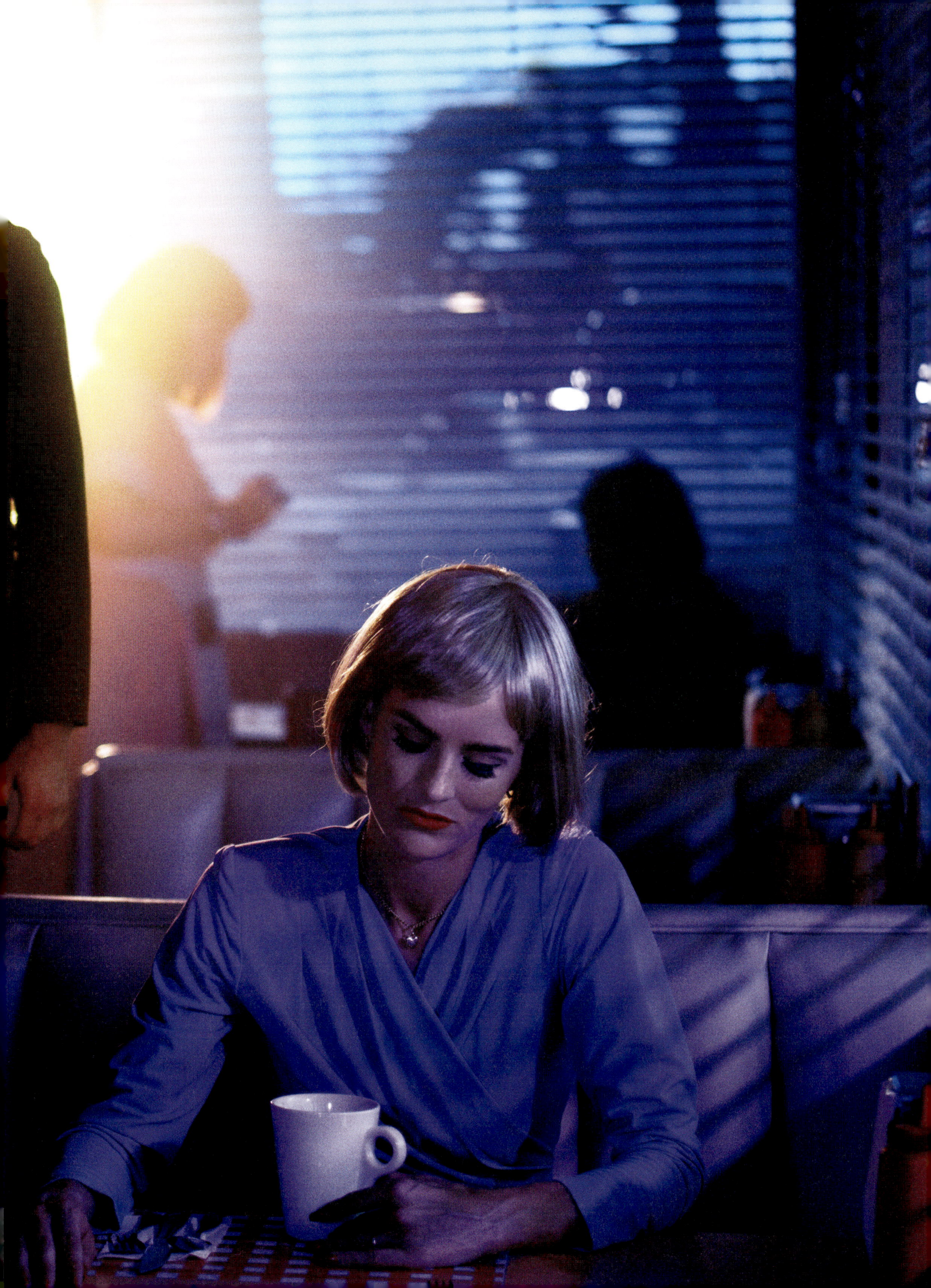

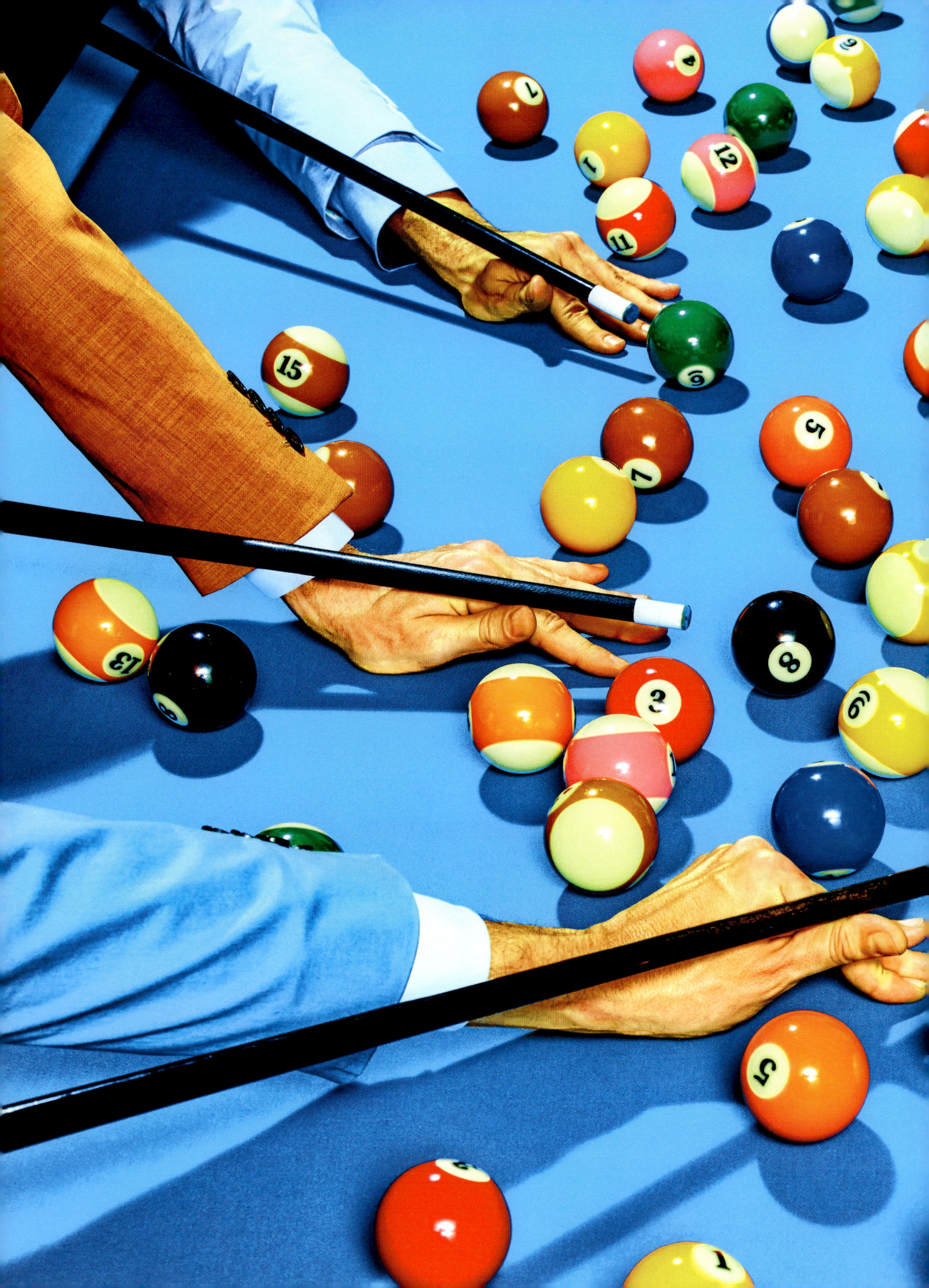

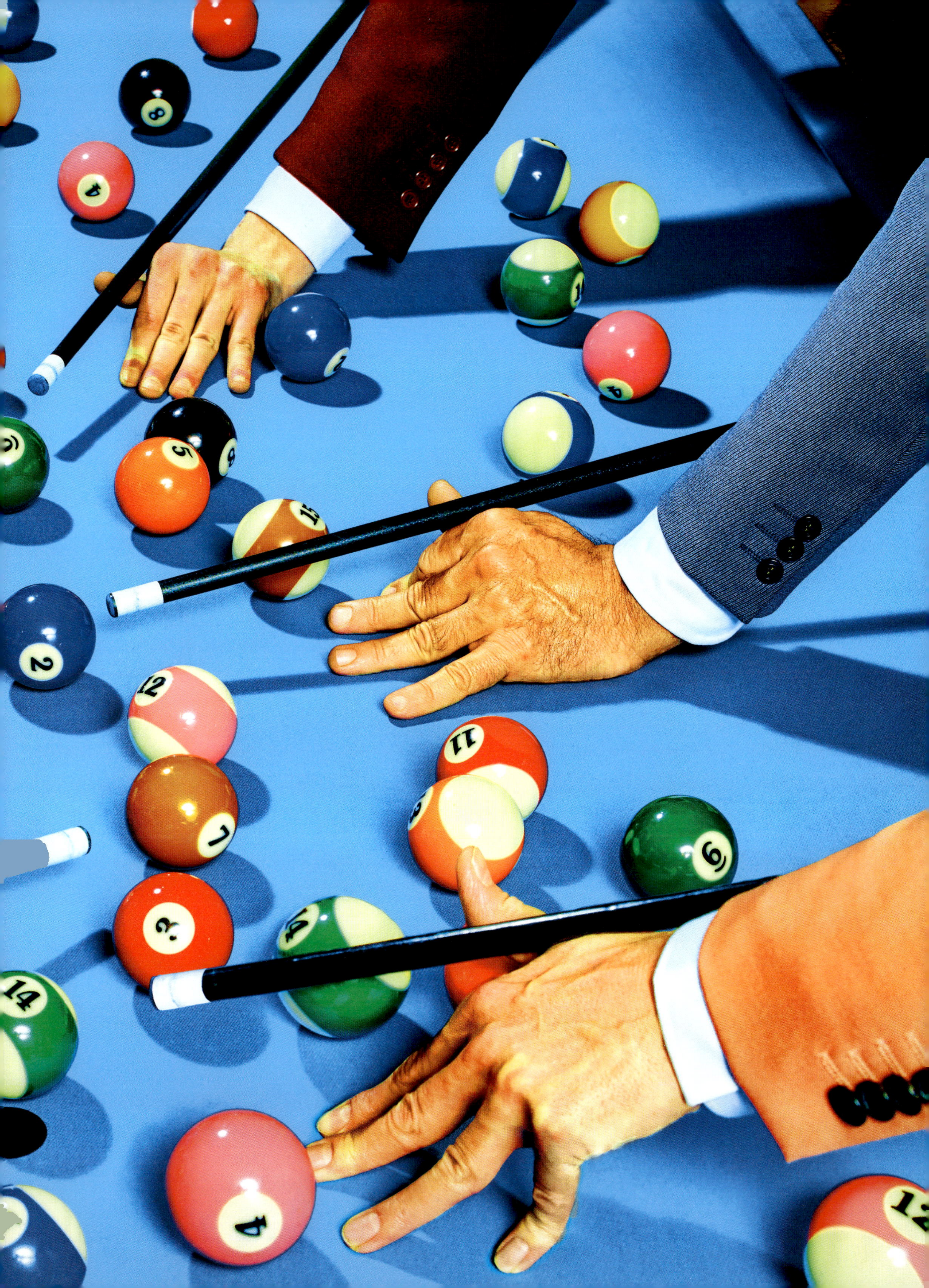

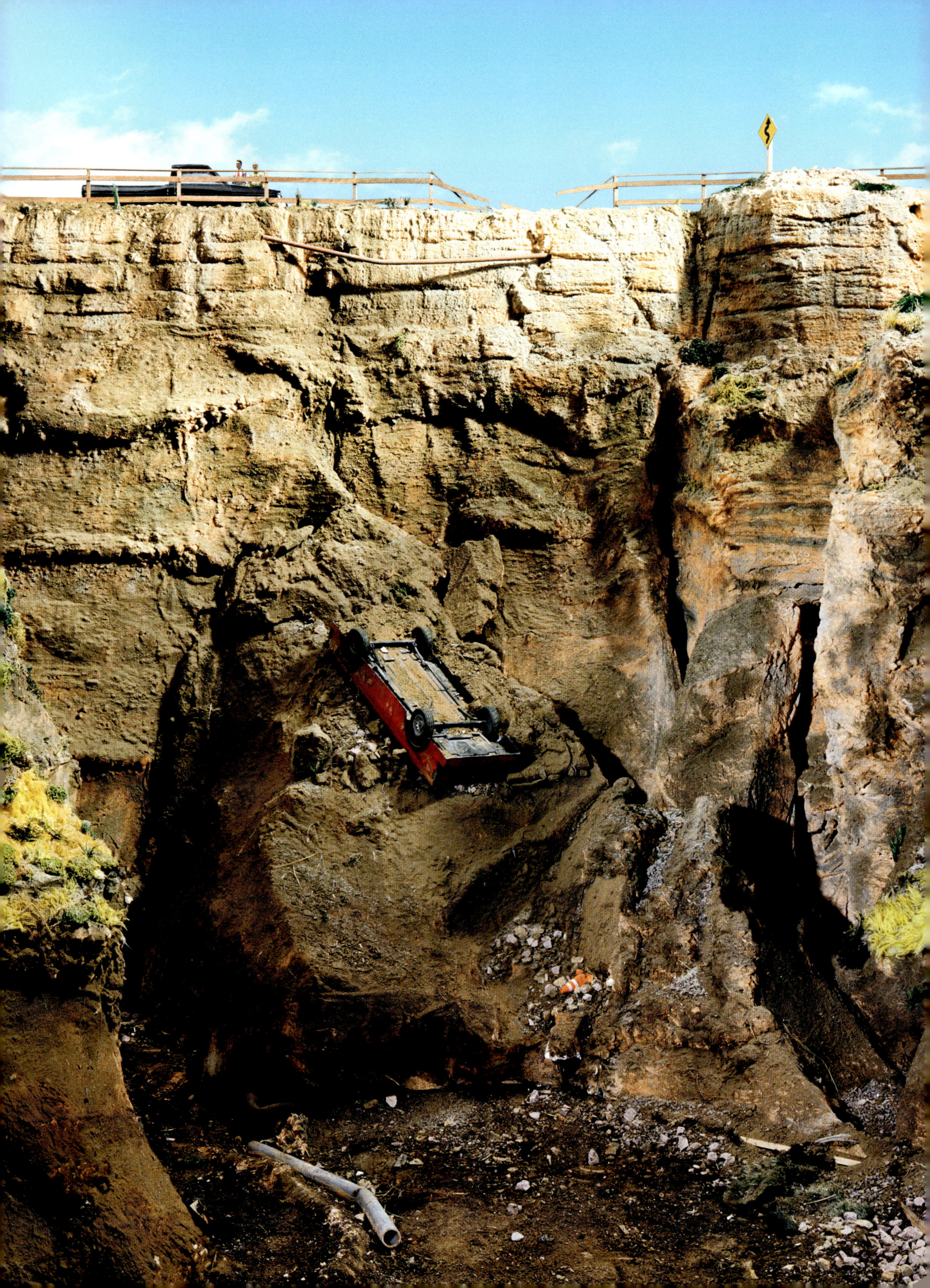

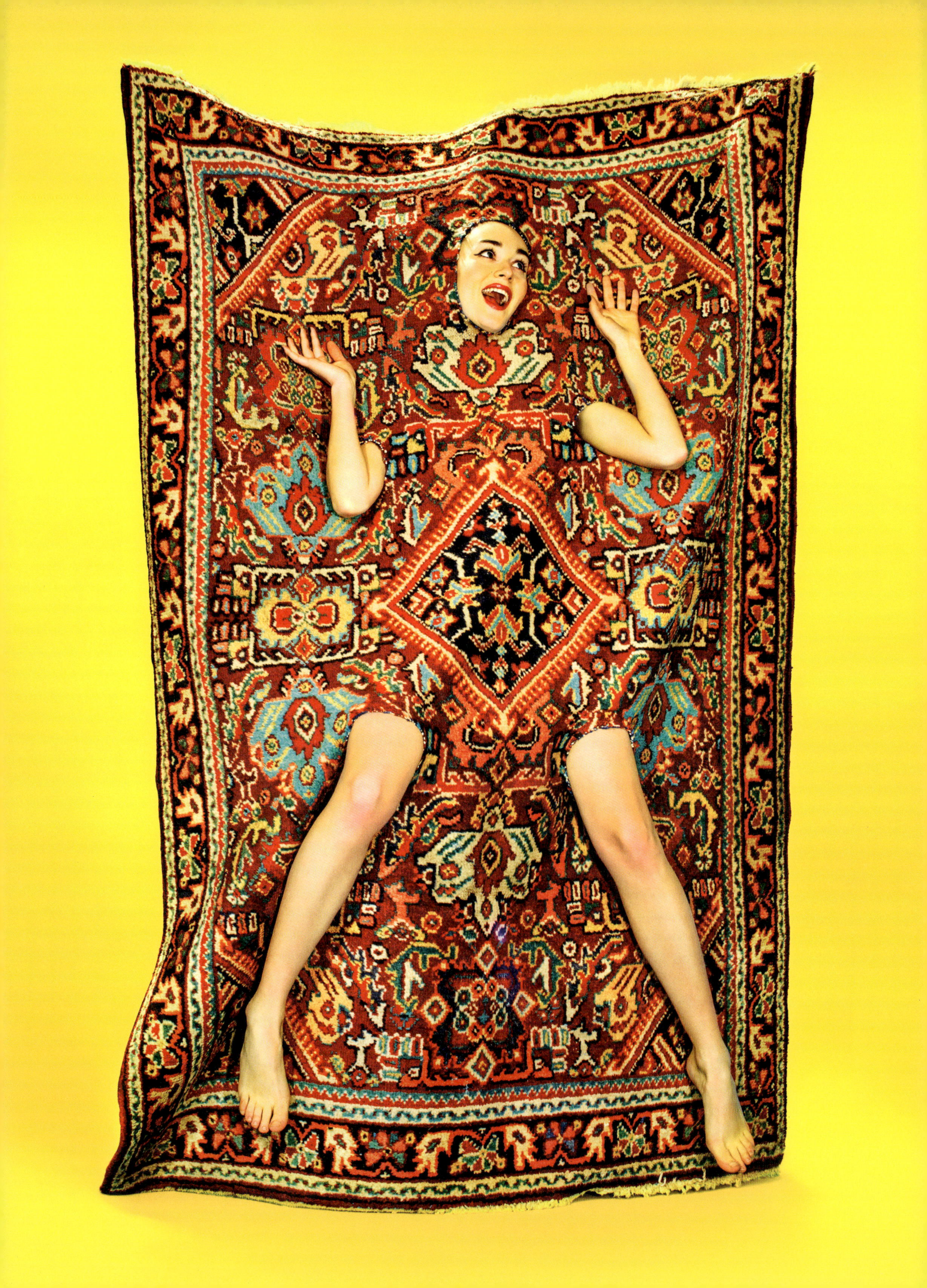

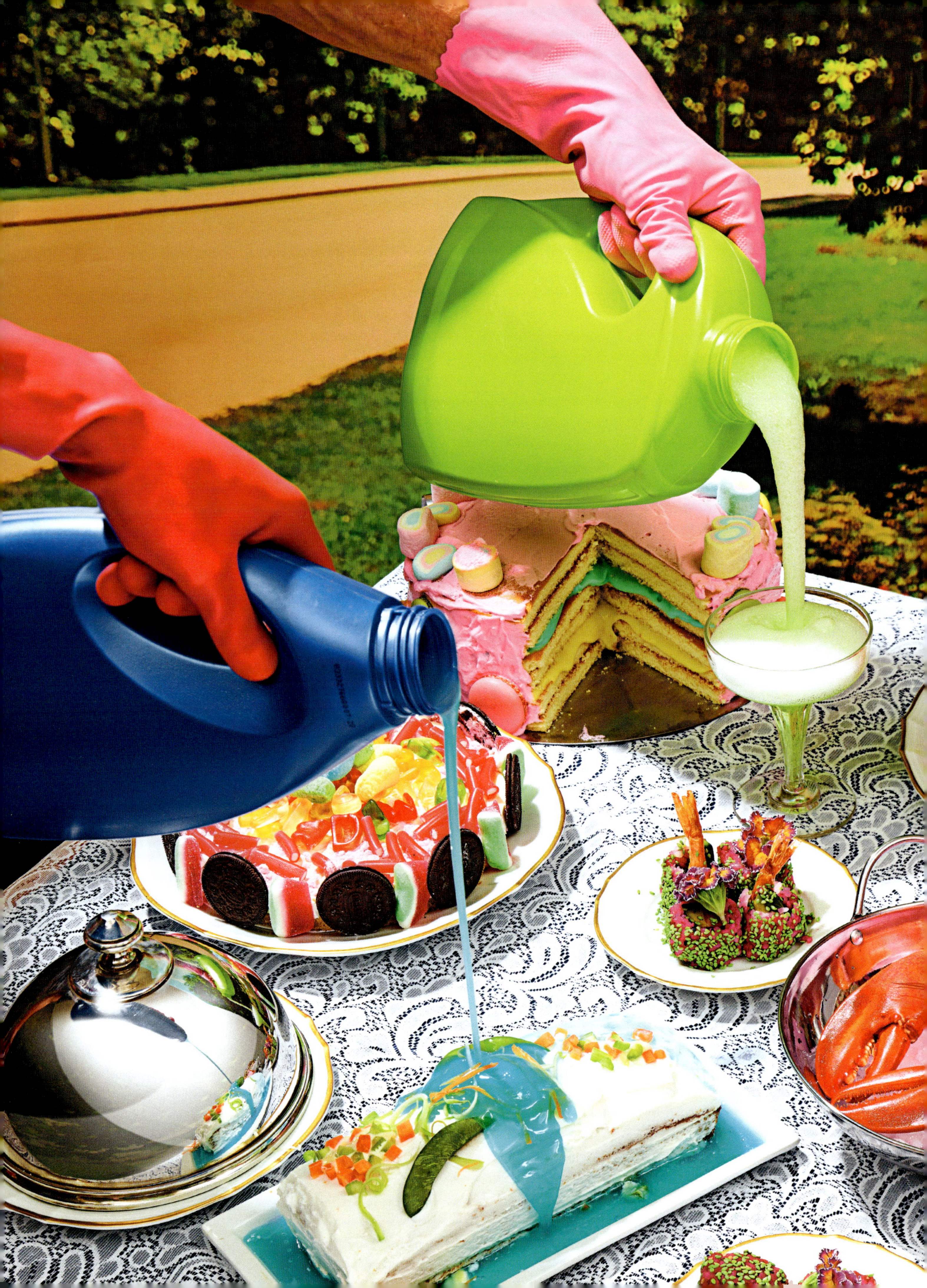

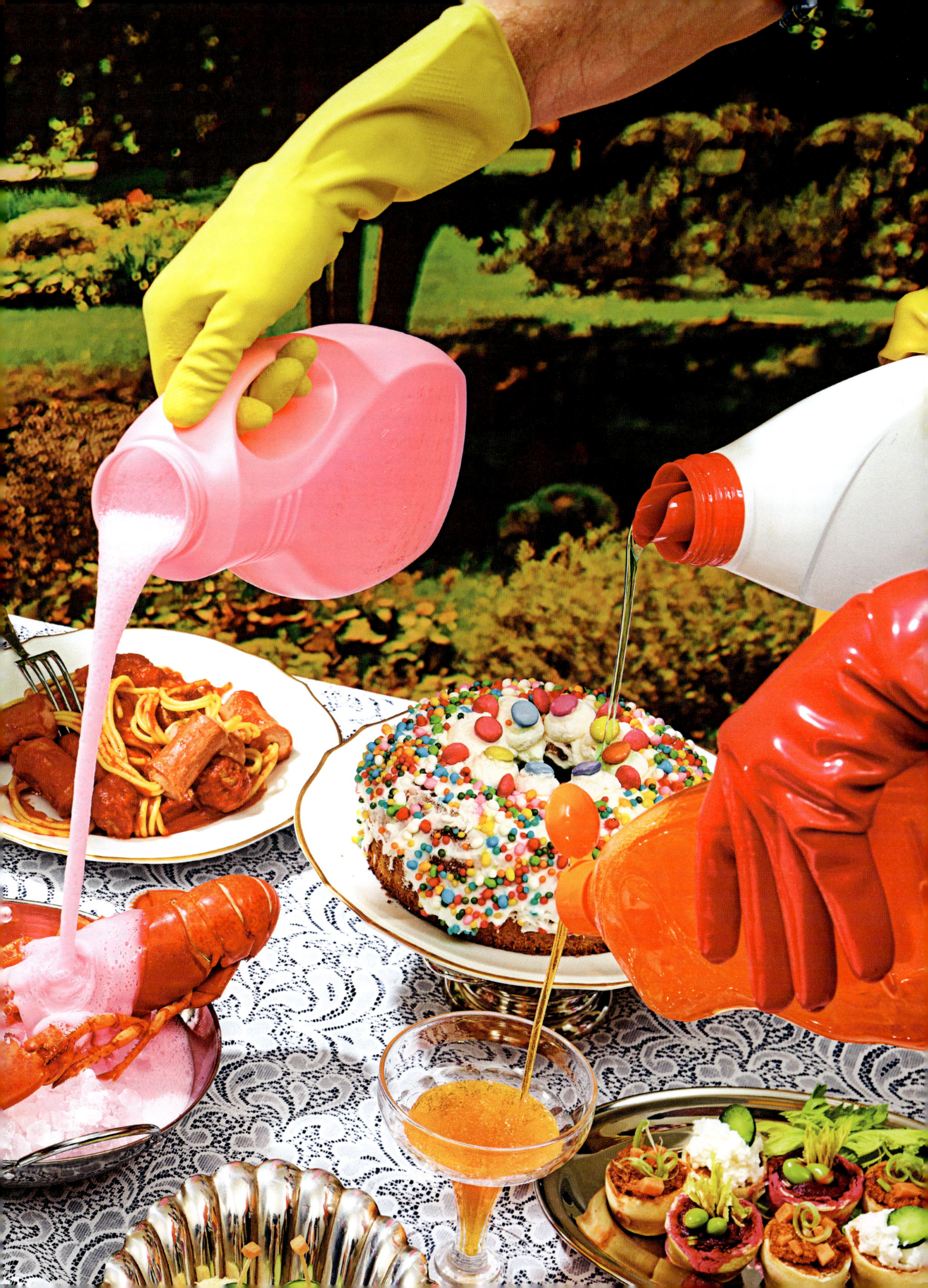

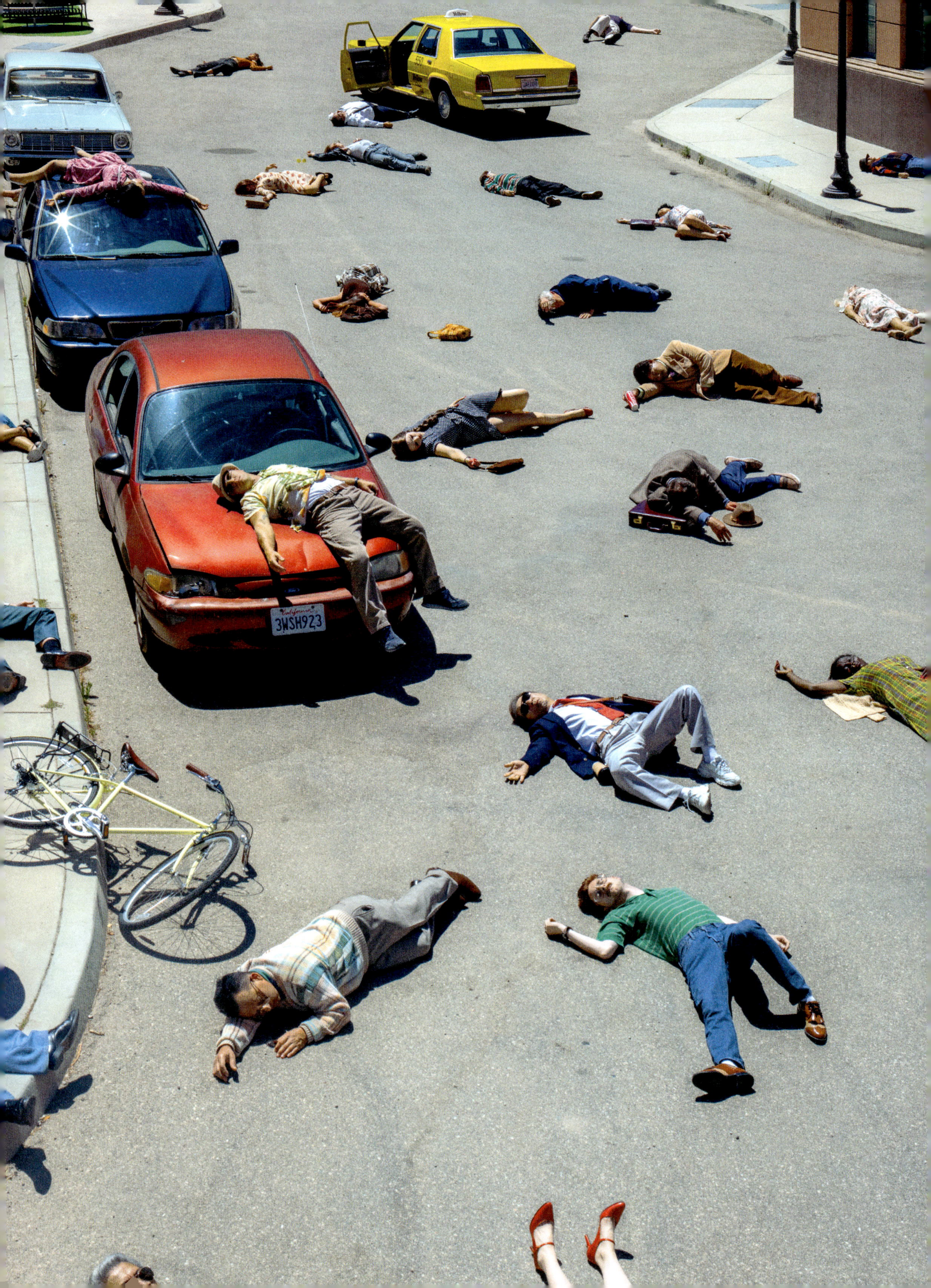
3WSH923

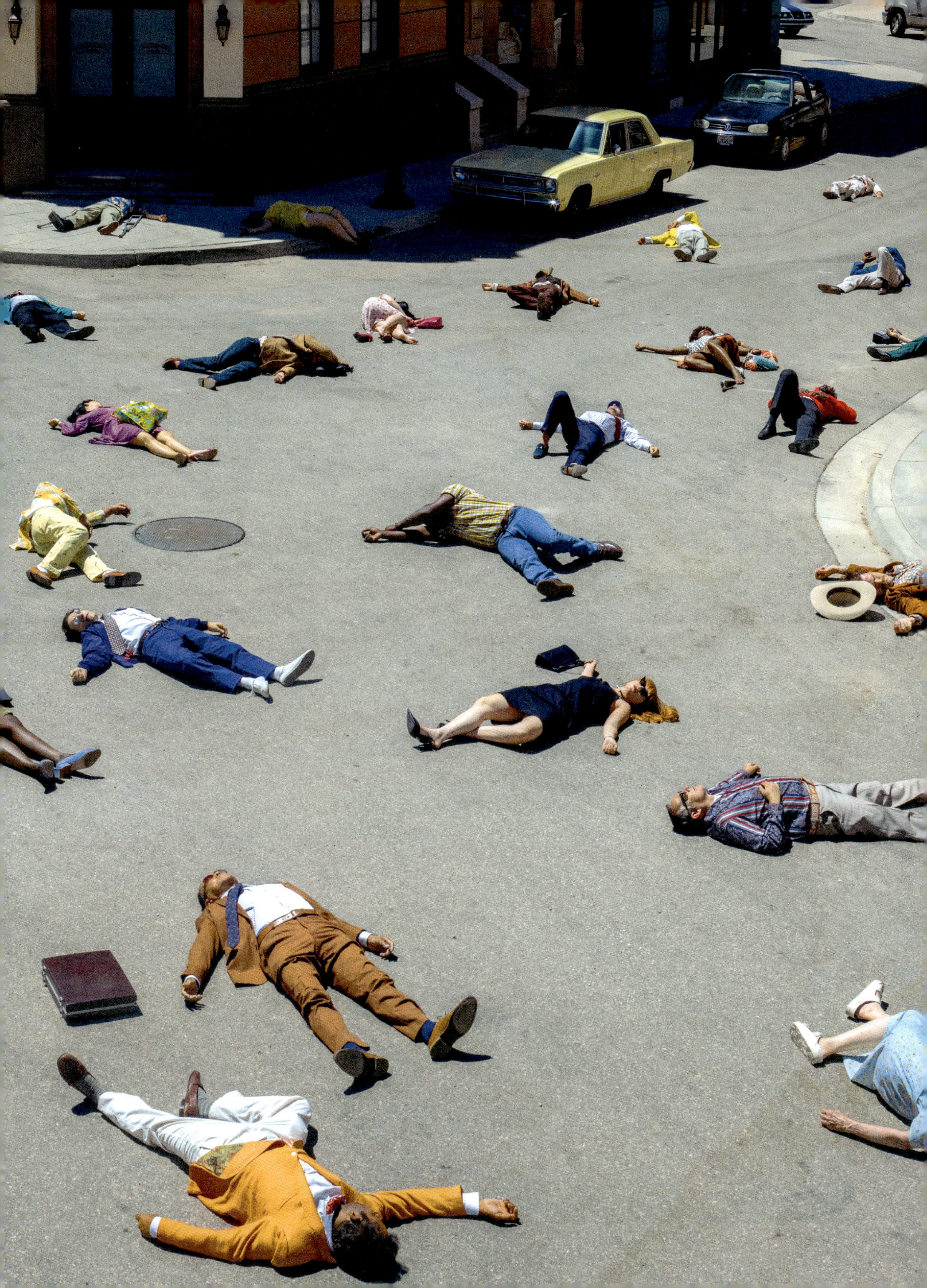

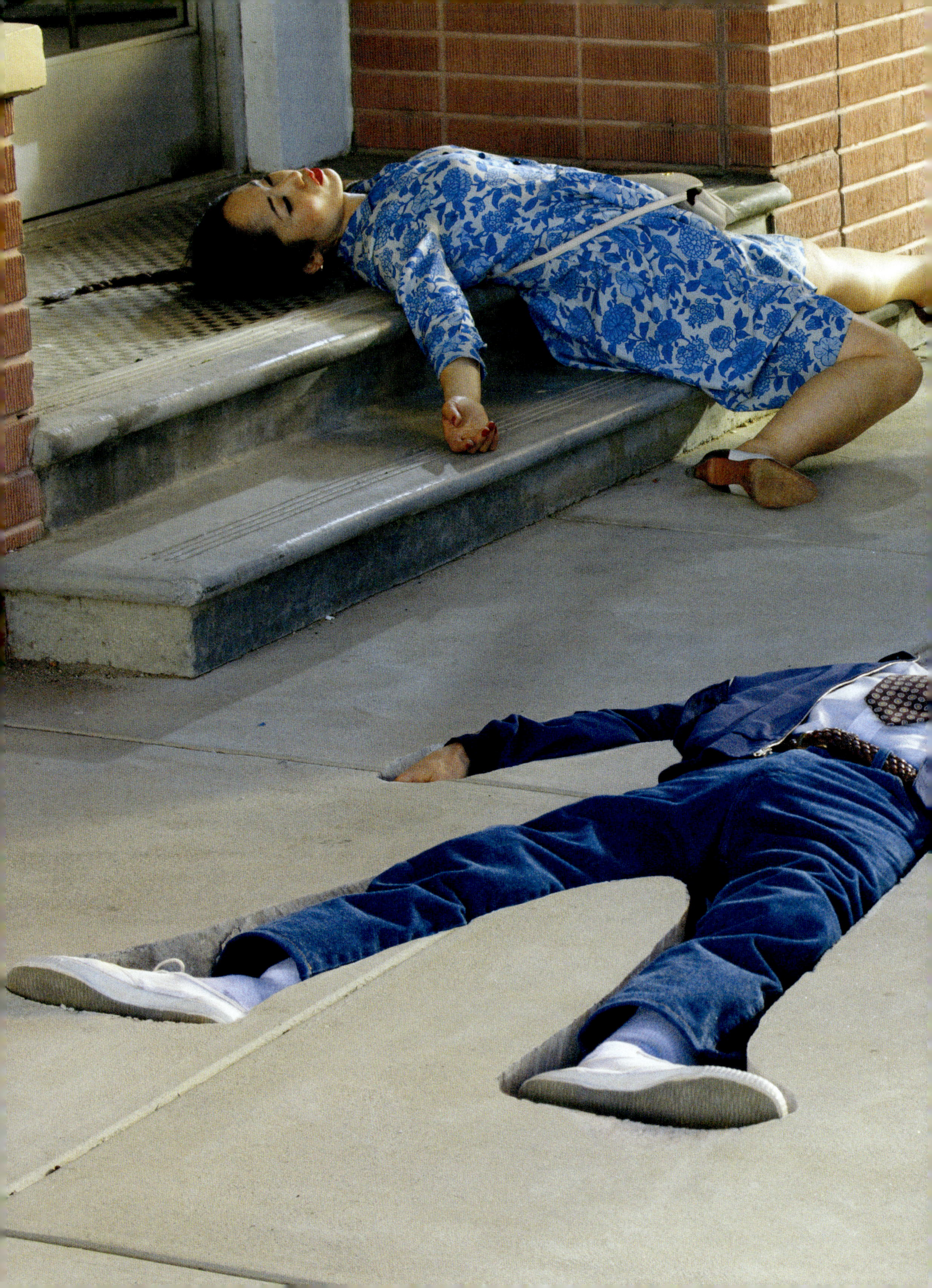

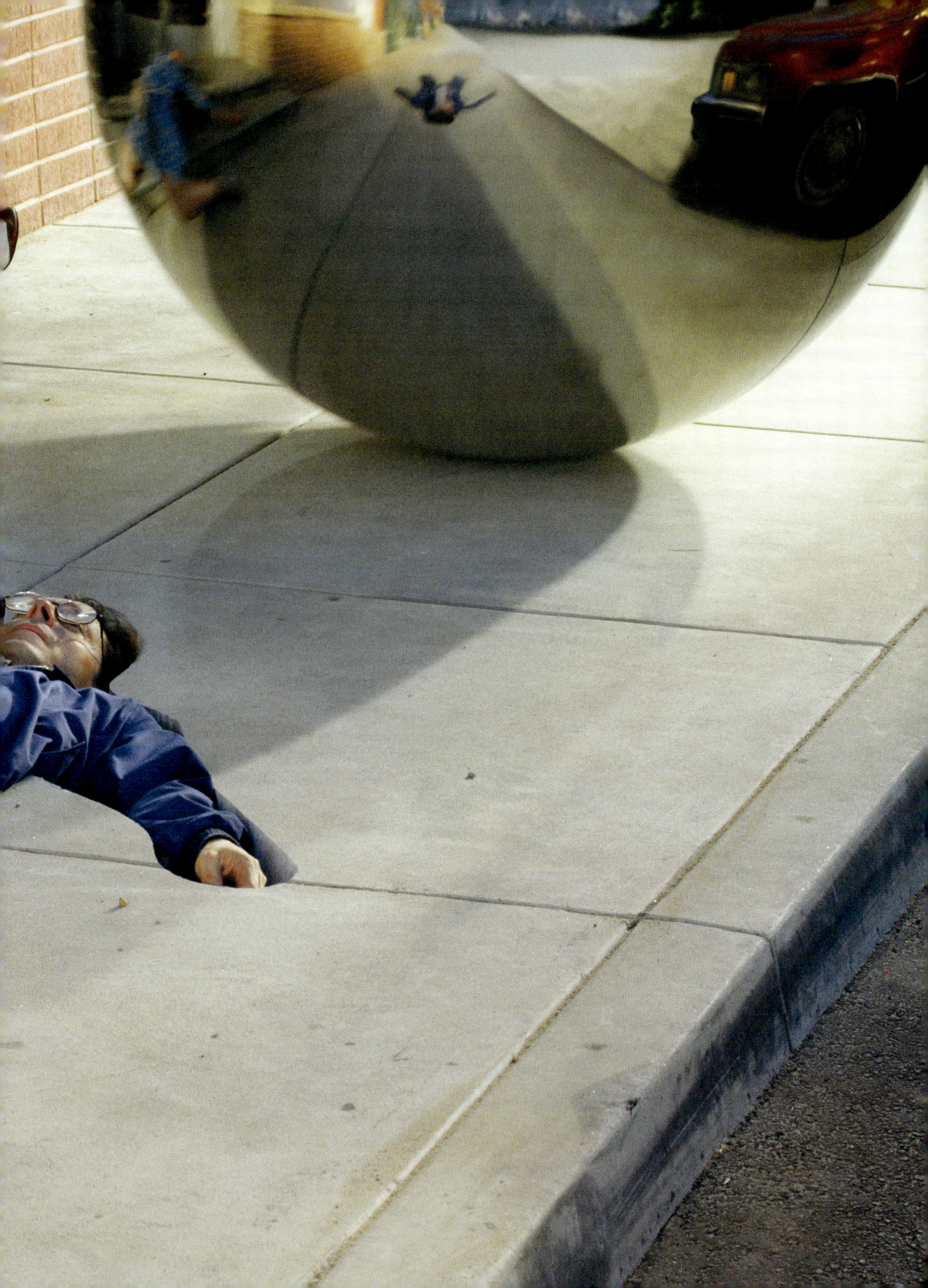

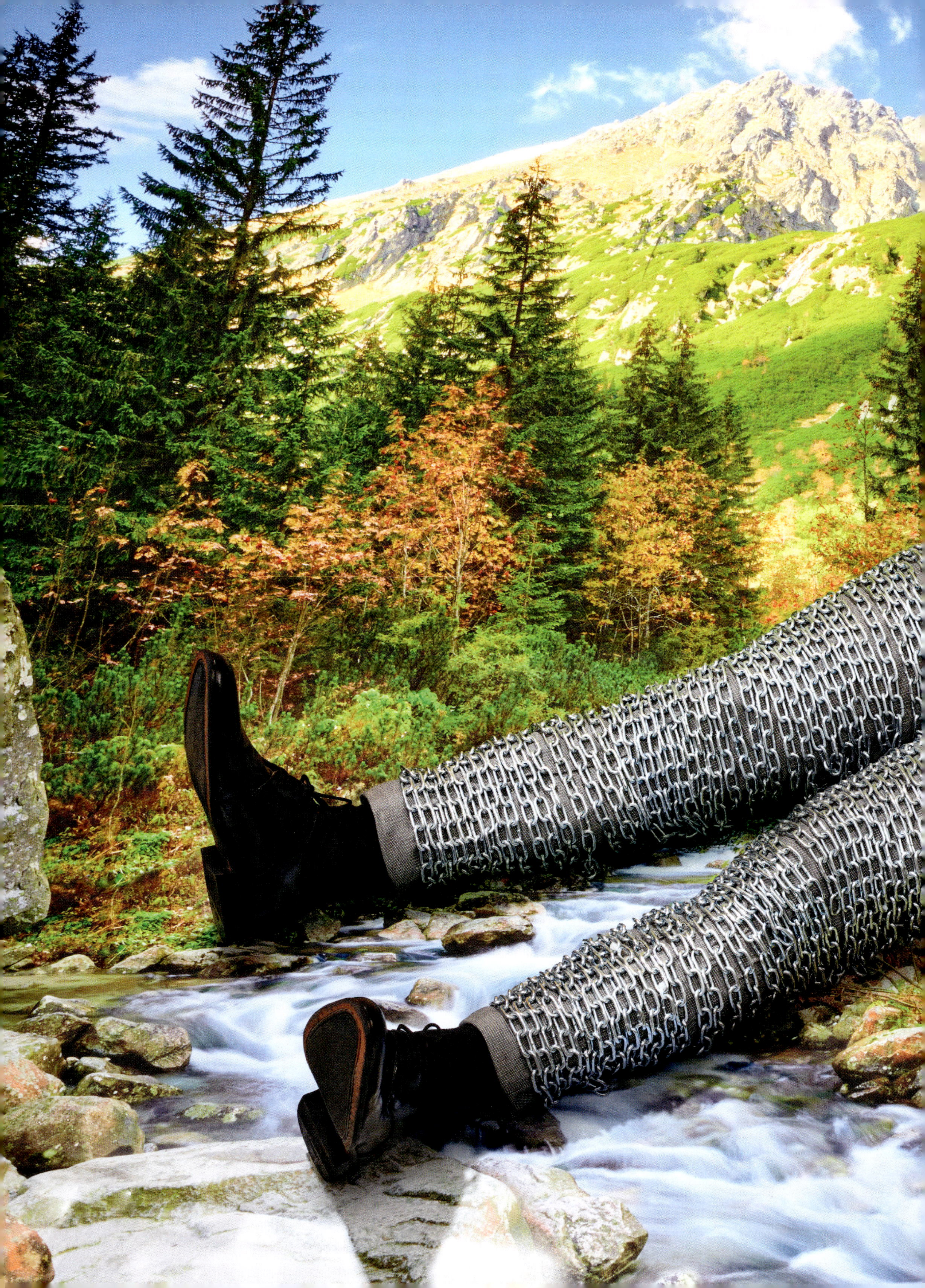

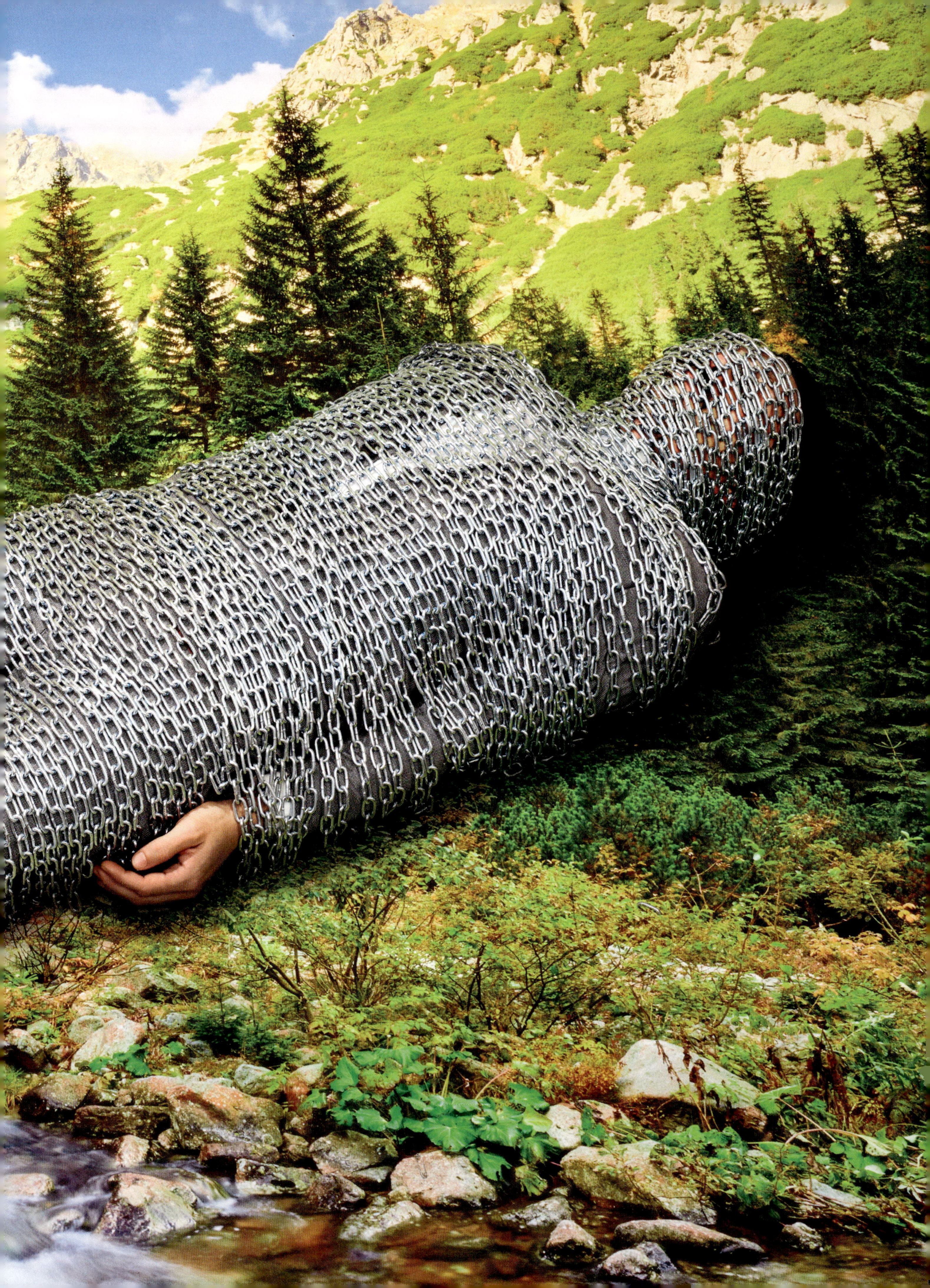

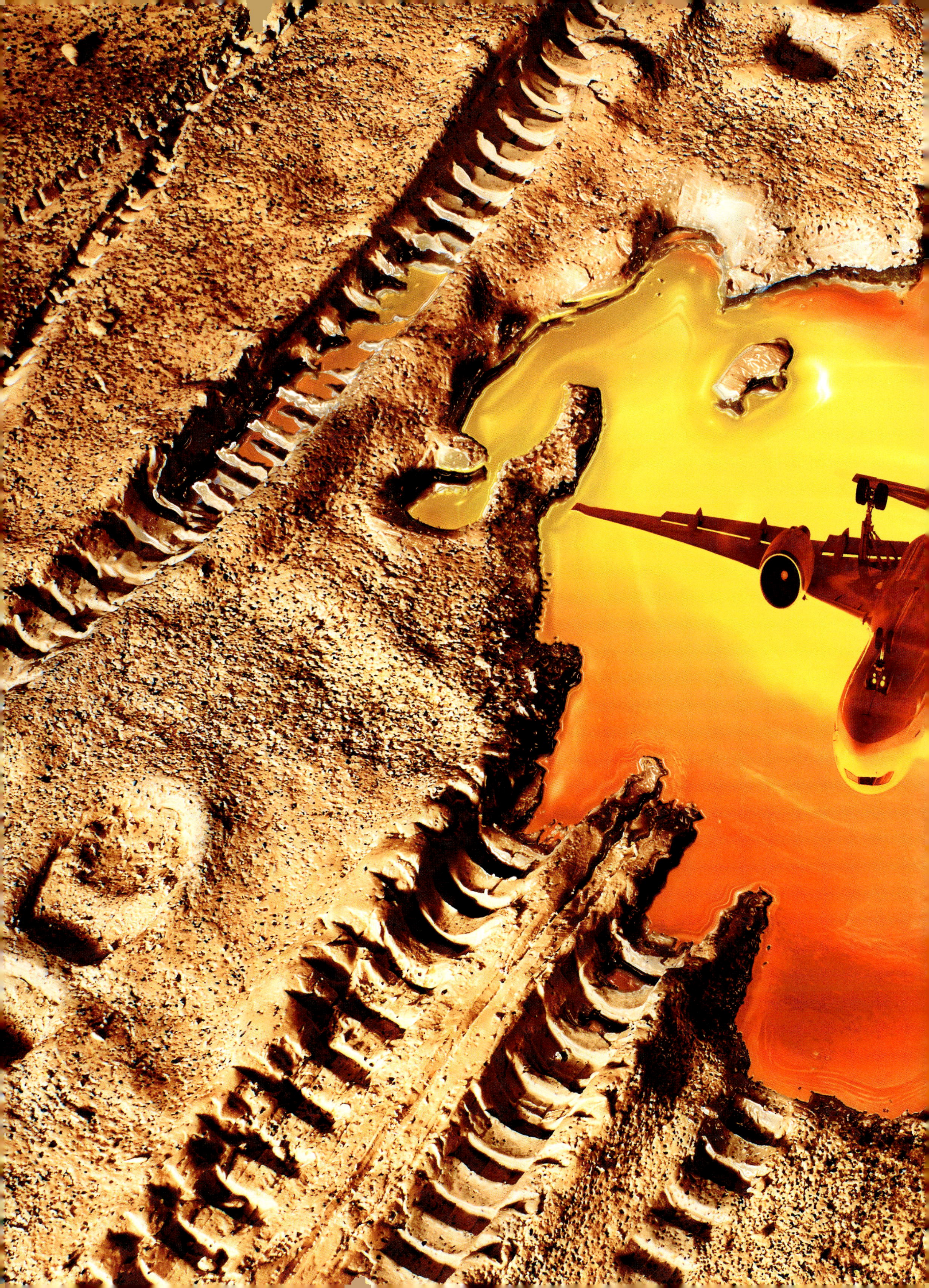

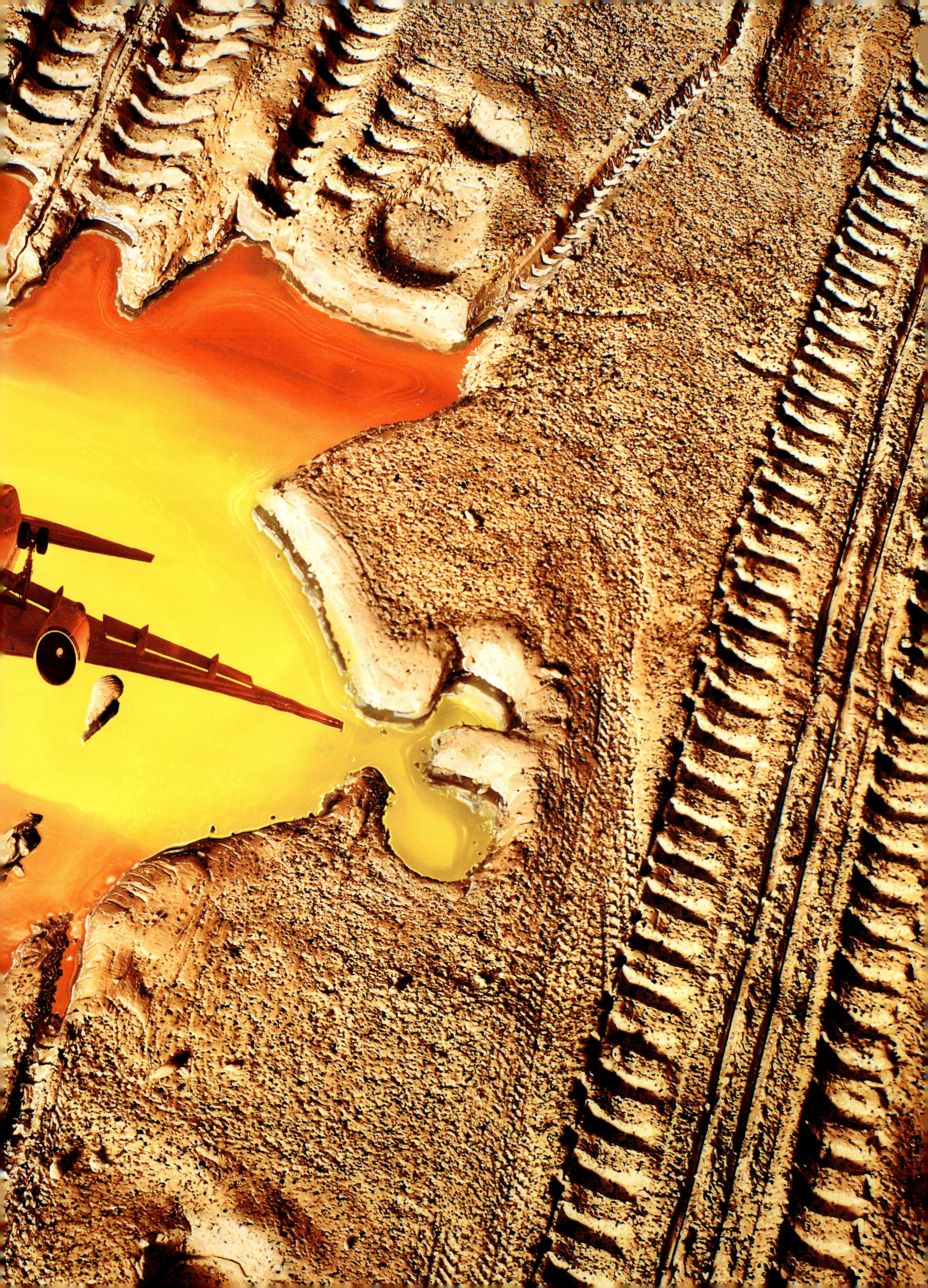

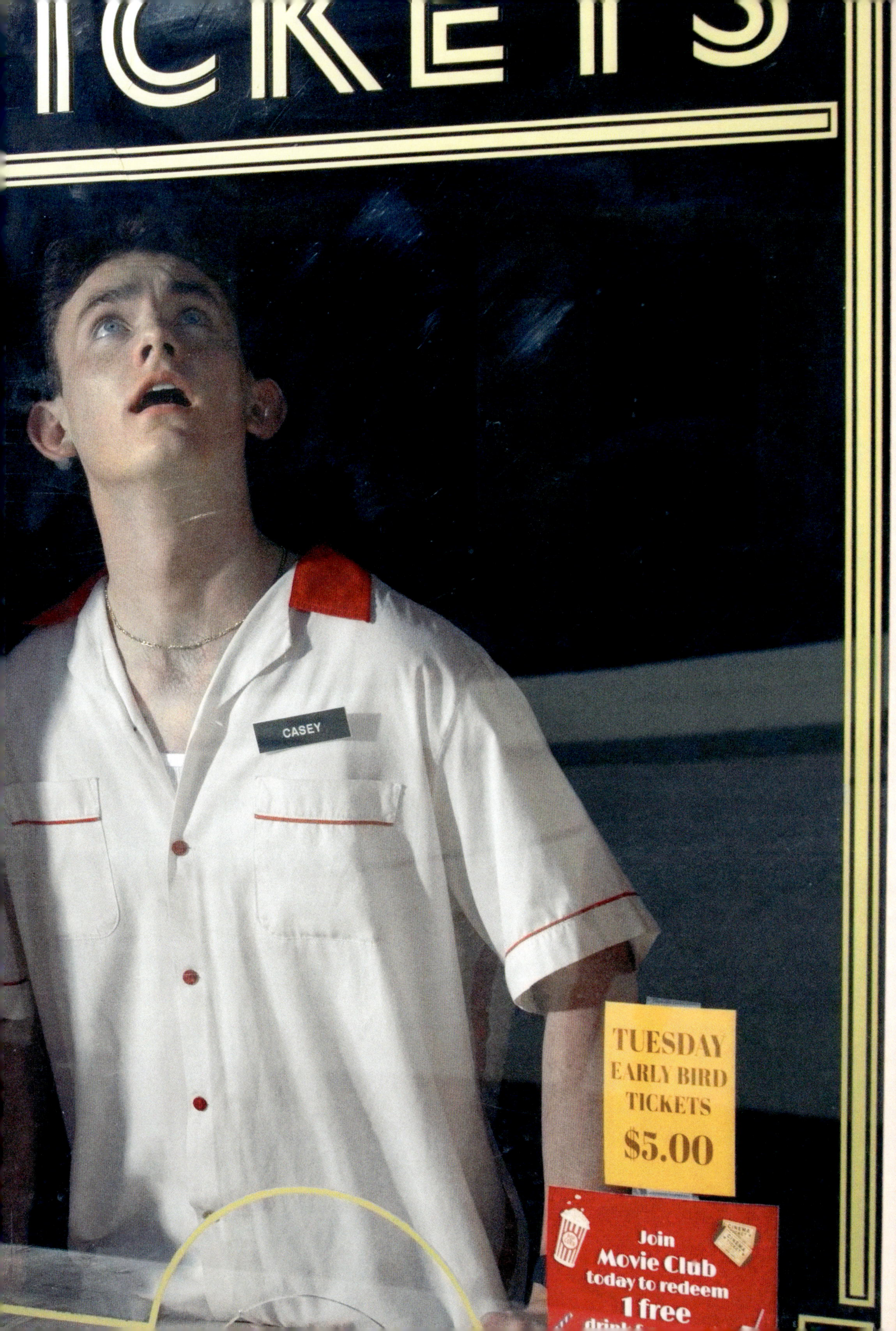
ICKETS
CASEY
TUESDAY
EARLY BIRD
TICKETS
$5.00
Join
Movie Club
today to redeem
1 free

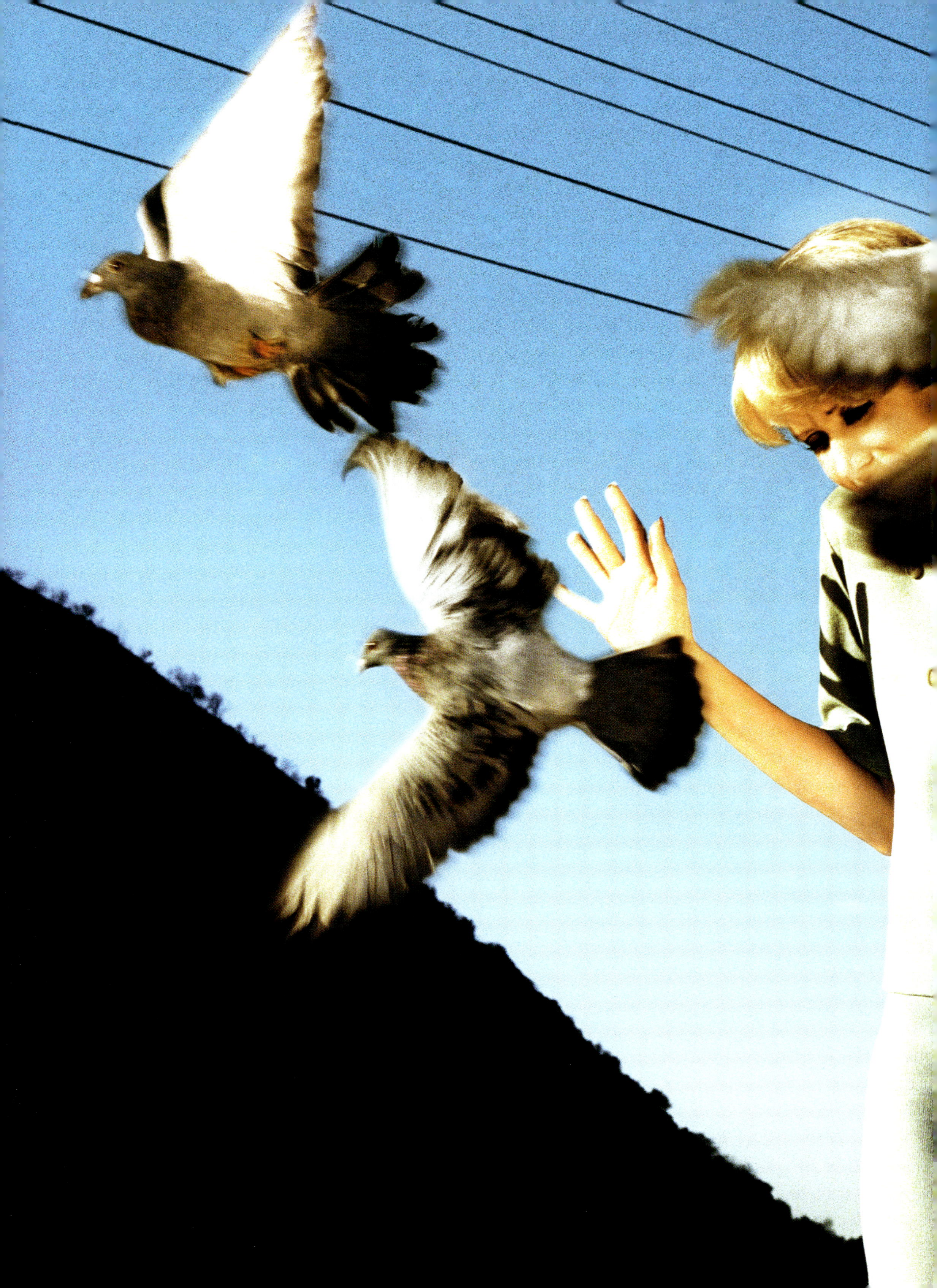

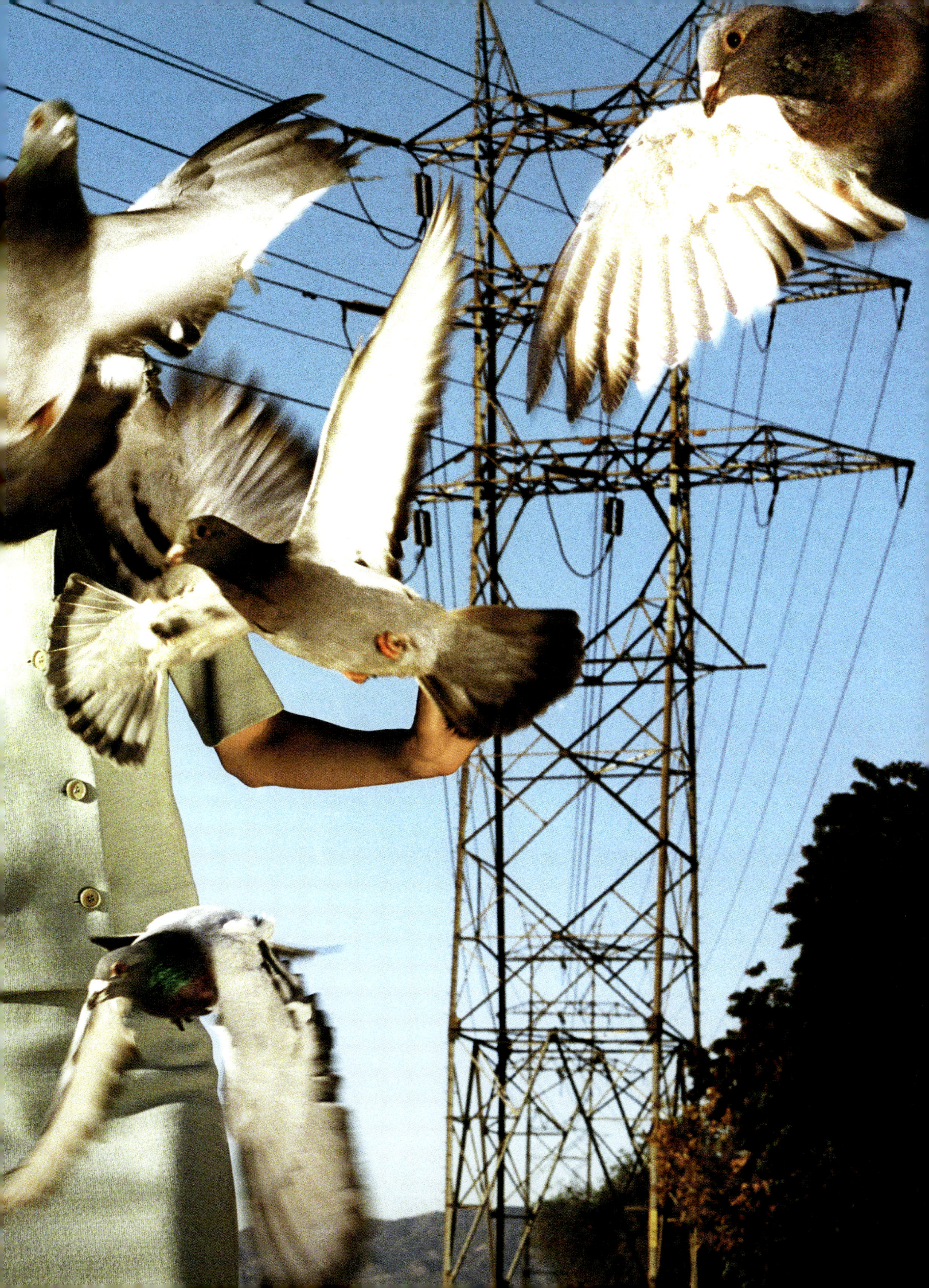

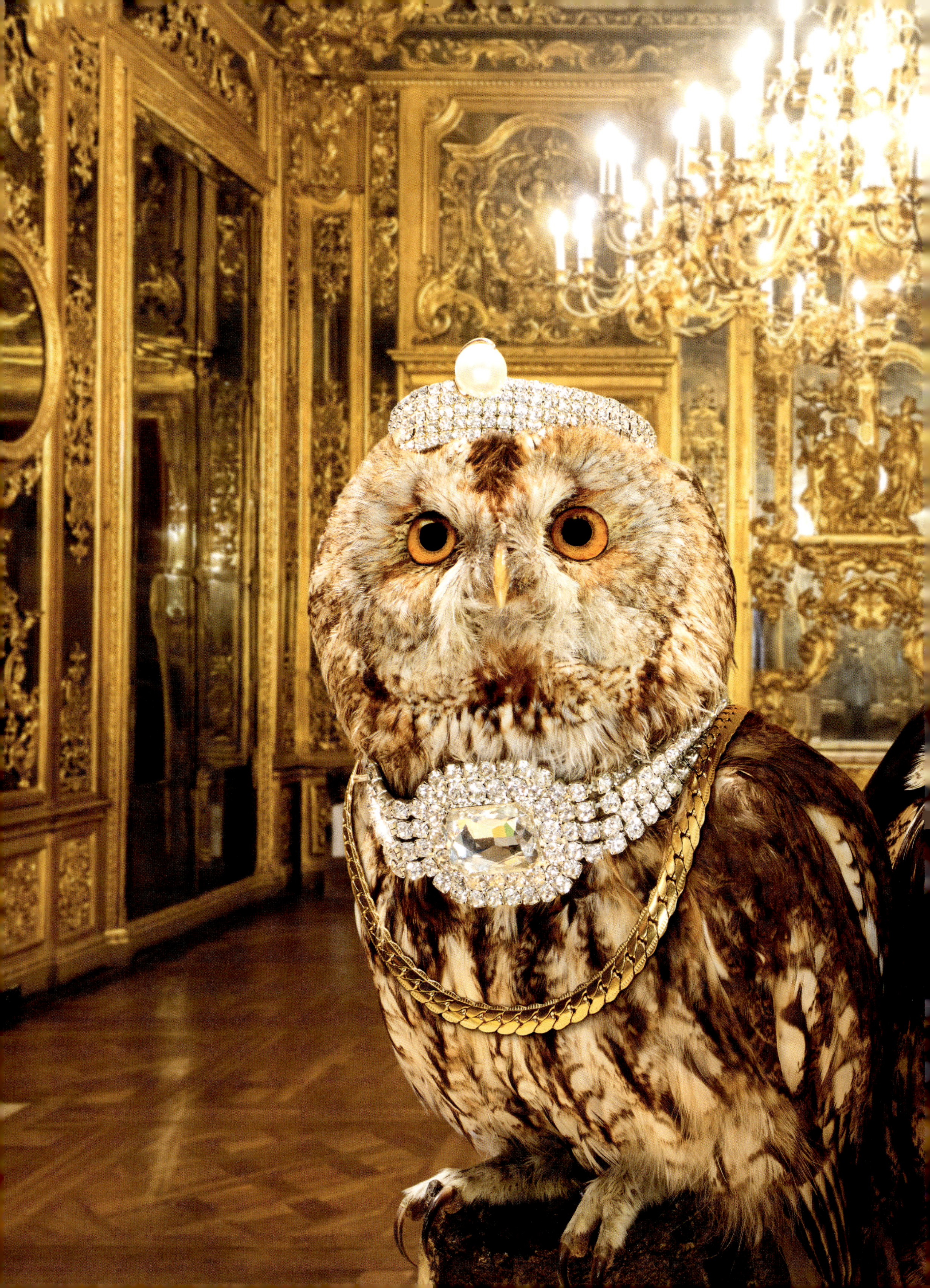

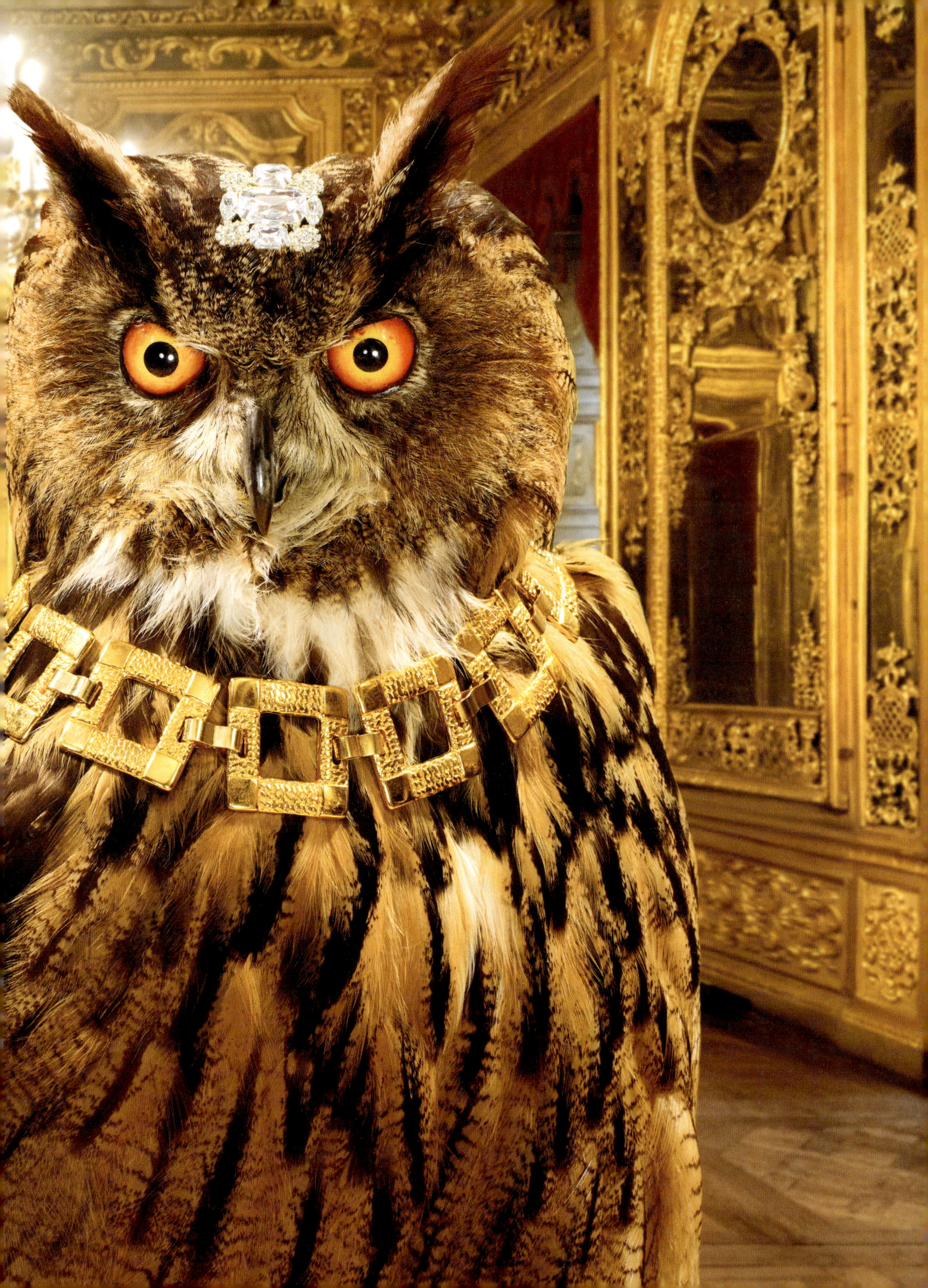

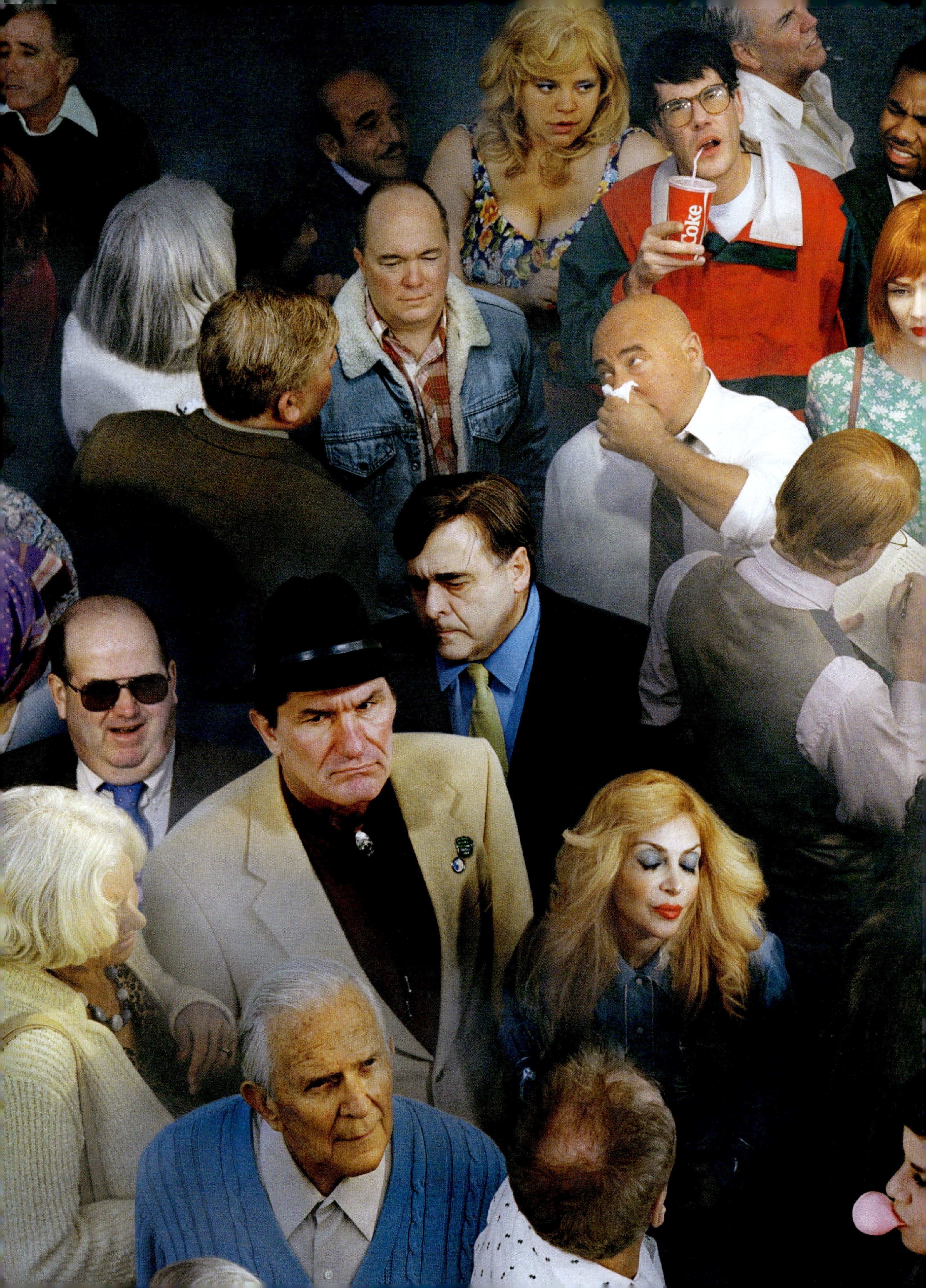
Coke

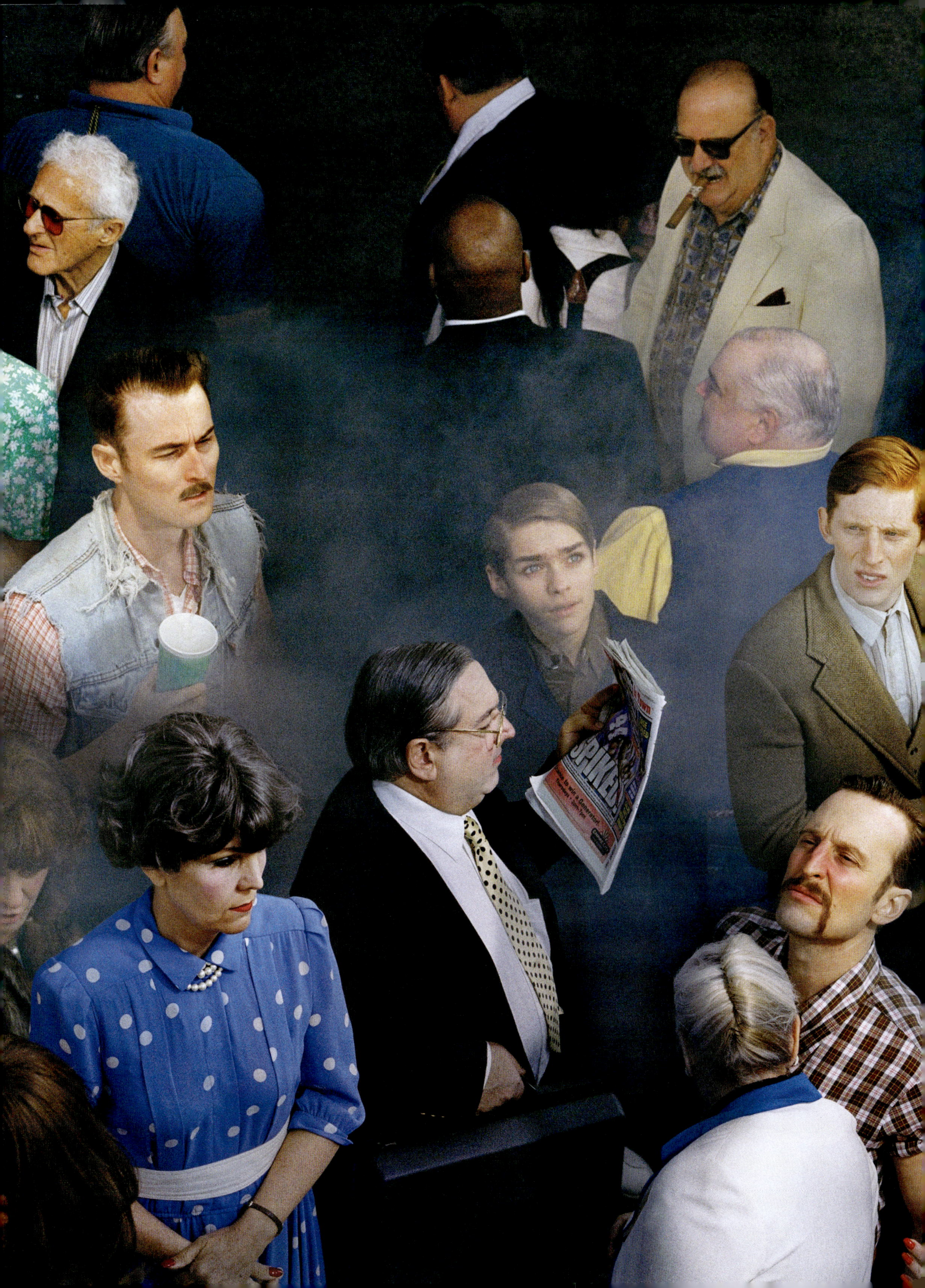
SPIKED!

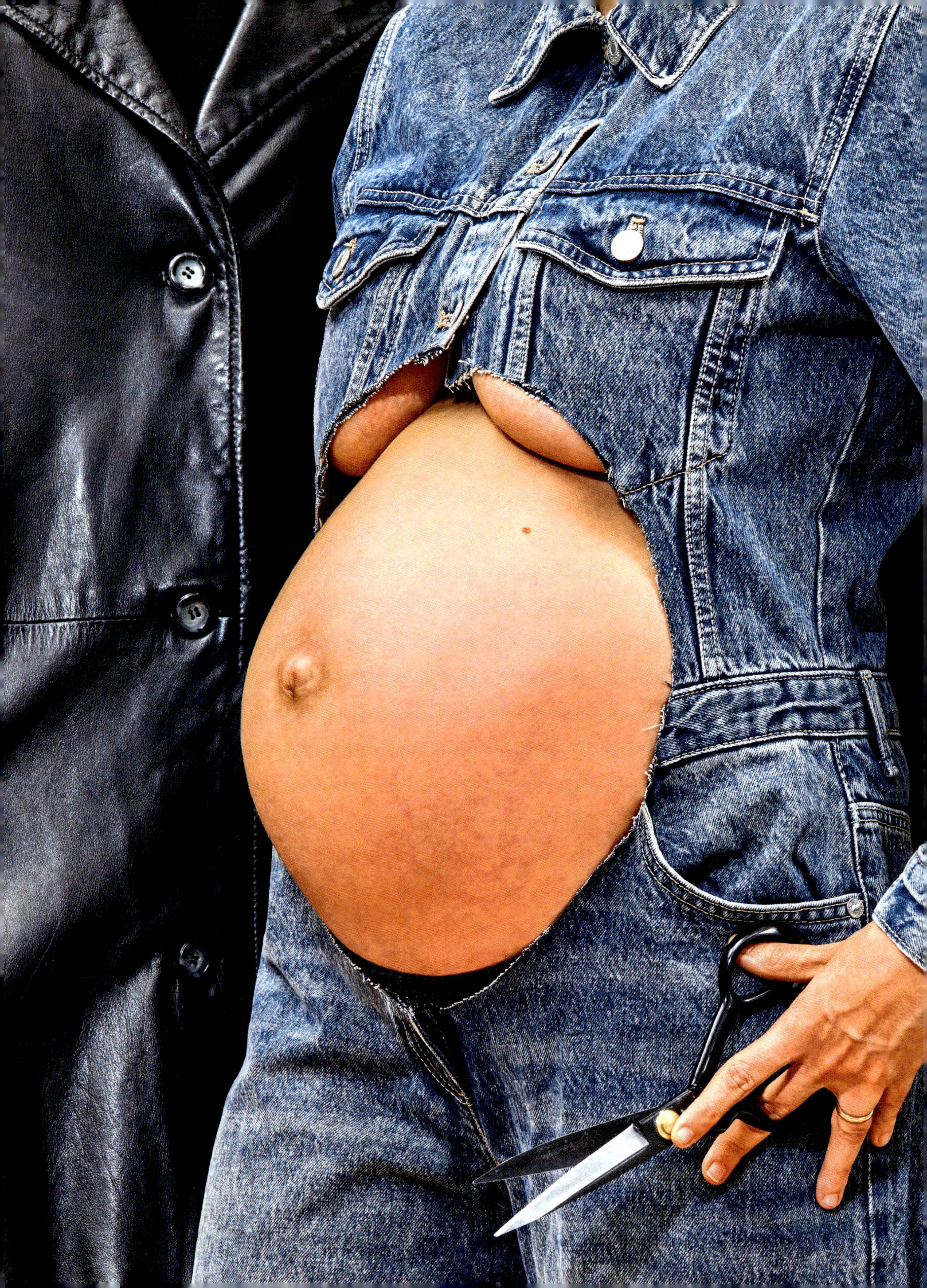